TOILET
TRAINING
The
Brazelton Way

also by T. Berry Brazelton, M.D.

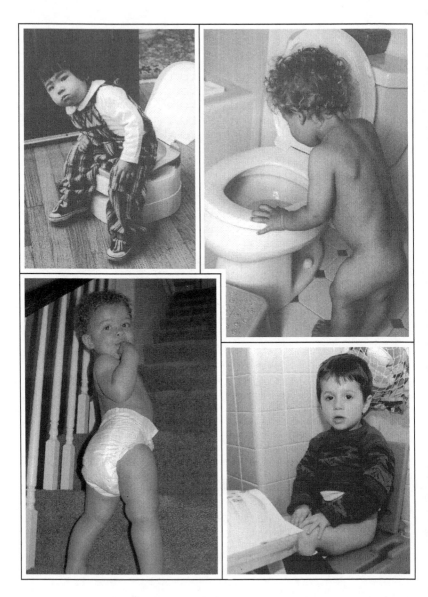

TOILET TRAINING
The
Brazelton Way

T. Berry Brazelton, M.D.
Joshua D. Sparrow, M.D.

A MERLOYD LAWRENCE BOOK
LIFELONG BOOKS • DA CAPO PRESS
A Member of the Perseus Books Group

PHOTO CREDITS

**Photographs on pages xx, 48 and title page [upper right and upper left]
by Janice Fullman**

**Photograph on title page [lower right]
by Dorothy Littell Greco**

**Photographs on page 8 and title page [lower left]
by Marilyn Nolt**

Text design by Trish Wilkinson
Set in 11-point Adobe Garamond by the Perseus Books Group

Cataloging-in-Publication data for this book is available from the Library of
Congress.

First Da Capo Press edition 2004
ISBN 13: 978-0-7382-0920-3
ISBN 10: 0-7382-0920-1

Published by Da Capo Press
A Member of the Perseus Books Group
http://www.dacapopress.com

Da Capo Press books are available at special discounts for bulk pur-
chases in the U.S. by corporations, institutions, and other organiza-
tions. For more information, please contact the Special Markets De-
partment at the Perseus Books Group, 11 Cambridge Center,
Cambridge, MA 02142, or call (800) 255–1514 or (617) 252–5298,
or e-mail special.markets@perseusbooks.com.

5 6 7 8 9—08 07

To the children and parents
who have taught us so much through the years

Contents

Foreword

It is a great honor to write the foreword to this book since my work with families on toilet training their children has been so profoundly influenced by Dr. T. Berry Brazelton. Dr. Brazelton, through his Touchpoints Model, has taught so many of us to observe the child's cues and respect the child's perspective, as well as to understand the normal predictable times (touchpoints) when a child's behavior falls apart prior to a burst in development. He also has taught us to expect that these touchpoints will cause parents to feel vulnerable. Since the average age for toilet training is now 3 years, a child experiences many touchpoints while developing toileting skills. Needless to say the child's cues can be very confusing to adults.

For many years I was a nurse practitioner in a suburban pediatric practice with four pediatricians. I remember the parents' struggles as they balanced competing needs and competing advice about how to toilet train their children. It was then, as I struggled with how to support parents, that I first read about and saw Dr. Brazelton and became a student of his methods. After many years, I left primary care to work with Dr. Brazelton and to focus more in depth on how to help parents understand their child's point of view and particularly to support them as they face their children's toilet training difficulties.

At Children's Hospital, Boston I worked in a specialty clinic with families who were having trouble toilet training their children. Together with a psychologist and a pediatric fellow, I designed Toilet School, a successful program that is now in its eighth year. One approach that we found effective was a six-week program in which parents and their children (between the ages of 4 and 6 and who were not toilet trained) met in separate groups for one hour each week. Parents compared notes and discovered that they dominated their children's training. Children supported each other and began to feel in control of their own bodies. By taking one step at a time the parents supported their children in taking over the task of toilet training. The program included both typically developing children as well as developmentally challenged children. Through Toilet School, I learned a great deal about the child's, the parent's, and the professional's perspectives.

One child told me a story about a raccoon in her toilet who didn't want her to poop. Another child told me how he "tricked his poop" by cutting a hole in his diaper before he put it on so that the BM went into the toilet but it (the BM) thought it was going into his diaper. I learned a great deal about the creative thinking of the 4- to 6-year-old. Their imaginary excursions helped them to make sense of their expanding world and the problems that confronted them, like not being able to use the toilet.

Parents told me of their confusion in understanding what their role should be. They told how they received advice that didn't fit for them or conflicted with their family methods of toilet training. They described being told to follow their child's cues without help in recognizing these, and they described their frustration and anger when they felt like failures because they were unable to help their child become toilet trained.

Physicians, nurses, childcare, and early education professionals told me of their frustration in trying to support parents. They had neither the time, they said, nor the training to give collaborative, rather than prescriptive, support to parents.

The Touchpoints model of predictable parent/child vulnerability and regressions informed the methods used in Toilet School. In the parent group, a collaborative approach is stressed and the child's cues are discussed. In the child group, play is used to empower each child and reduce his or her stress.

Many of the issues that bring families to Children's Hospital's Toilet School are preventable. For instance, constipation can interfere with toilet training. Children avoid pain. If they think a BM will hurt they hold it back. Timing is also very important. If a child is learning something new like running, he may resist any toilet training lessons.

In this book, Drs. Brazelton and Sparrow help parents understand their child's perspective and give helpful ideas for structuring this universal task. Some children need more structure while others need less. This book helps parents understand just what their child needs and promote their child's self-esteem through a positive toilet training experience.

The goal is for the child to say, "I did it myself!" Children who feel that they themselves accomplished the task of independent toileting are inspired by this experience to accomplish the next task. If they are unable to accomplish this challenging task, they may withdraw or deny that they care and begin to develop a sense of not being capable. Parents who are unable to help their child learn toileting skills may get frustrated and angry, or feel incapable as parents. Once again we can rely on Drs. Brazelton and Sparrow for their insights so that these negative reactions can be avoided and parents can support their children's success in toilet training.

Ann Stadtler, M.S.N., C.P.N.P.
Founder of Toilet School, Children's Hospital, Boston
Director, Touchpoints Site Development and Support

Preface

Ever since I wrote the first *Touchpoints* book, published in 1992, I have been asked by parents and professionals all over the country to write some short, easy-to-read books about the common challenges that parents face as they raise their children. Among the most common are crying, discipline, sleep, toilet training, and feeding.

In my years of pediatric practice, families have taught me that problems in these areas often arise predictably as a child develops. In these short books I have tried to address the everyday problems that parents are bound to encounter as their children regress just before they make their next developmental leap. Each book describes these "touchpoints" so that parents can better understand their child's behavior. Each also offers practical suggestions on how parents can help their child master the challenges they face in these areas so that they can get back on track. I do not wish to burden parents with yet more advice but to help them reassert their own expertise.

In general these books focus on the challenges of the first years of life, though occasionally older children's issues are referred to. In the final chapters, special problems are discussed, though these short books are not intended to cover these topics exhaustively. Instead, we hope that these books will serve as easy-to-use guides for parents to turn to as they face their child's growing pains, or "touchpoints" that affect the critical areas of development.

As with *Touchpoints Three to Six,* I have invited Joshua Sparrow, M.D., to co-author these books with me, to add his perspective to mine. Though difficulties such as excessive crying, middle of the night wakings, temper tantrums, bedwetting, and food fights, for example, are both common and predictable, they make great demands on parents. These kinds of problems are for the most part temporary and not serious, yet without support and understanding, they can overwhelm a family and send a child's development seriously off course. It is our hope that the straightforward information provided in these books will help prevent those unnecessary derailments, and provide reassurance for parents in times of uncertainty, so that the excitement and joy of helping a young child grow can be rekindled.

T. Berry Brazelton, M.D.
Joshua D. Sparrow, M.D.

TOILET
TRAINING
The
Brazelton Way

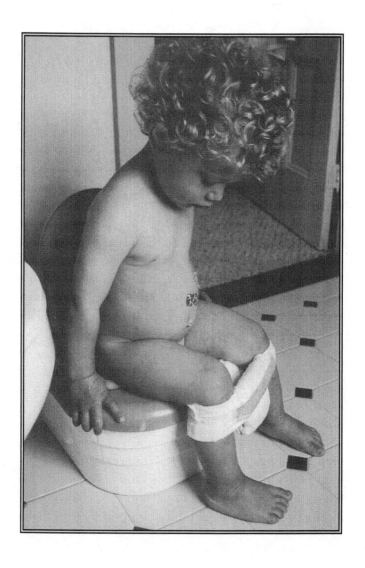

CHAPTER 1

Toilet Learning: The Child's Role

We don't always realize what we are asking of small children when we ask them to give in to toilet training. First, they must feel a bowel movement coming on. Then, they've got to hold onto their bowel movement, get where we tell them to go, sit down—and do it. Then, flush. After all that, they'll have to watch it disappear forever. They'll never see that part of themselves again!

What a lot to ask of a young child just at a time when he's trying to understand himself! At this age, children never know where their bowel movements have gone. This question may haunt them afterward. "Where is my poop? Why have they taken it away from me?"

Many years ago, a very large toilet, big enough for big children to climb in and all the way through, was constructed at the Children's Museum in Boston. They couldn't wait to see where their bowel movements had been going. Children 9, 10, and 11 years old lined up for blocks to try to find out where their "productions" had gone. They were still wondering, even at these ages.

The late Fred Rogers once asked a famous astronaut, Buzz Aldrin, to appear on his children's television show, *Mr. Rogers'*

Neighborhood. He invited his guest to answer all of the children's questions. One little boy said to the astronaut: "Do you get scared when you go up in space?" Mr. Aldrin bravely replied, "Well, I used to, but I don't anymore." A little girl asked, "Does your mommy get scared when you go up in space?" The astronaut answered, "Yep. She still does. Every time I come back to Earth, she's grateful." Then a 4-year-old boy had his turn: "What happens to your poop in space?" The astronaut turned beet red, shuffled around, and was unable to answer. The next question came as a relief.

Observations like these have helped me understand just how much we're asking of children in these formative years when they begin toilet training. We need to initiate the process with utmost respect for the child—and for his ultimate decision to comply. Training a small child to use the toilet must be taken in steps that respect his willingness to cooperate. Parents also need to feel comfortable discussing these issues, and recognizing feelings about toilet training left over from their own childhood.

In the 1960s I introduced "A Child Oriented Approach to Toilet Training" to my patients and their parents. They (and I) were ready. The incidence of toilet training failures was rising in our country (including toddlers who smeared their stools, children who were holding back on bowel movements, causing severe constipation, and older children with continued bedwetting). Back then it was common to employ rather rigid practices, pushing 1- and 2-year-olds to be trained. Parents tried to respond to a child's body's signals by rushing him to the toilet, well before he was aware enough of these signals to be an active participant.

If he complied, he was rewarded. If he didn't, he was reprimanded or punished.

It didn't work. Parents were trained in the method, but children were resistant. At this time in England, a rigid approach to toilet training was widespread: It was reported that 15 percent of 18-year-olds who were inducted into the service there were still wetting the bed. The other symptoms among children—withholding bowel movements, soiling, smearing stools—were also all too common. Many of these symptoms seemed to result from the child's resistance and resentment. Parental anxiety and the resulting pressure on children seemed to be interfering with the child's motivation for toilet training. It seemed to me that without the child's motivation, toilet training was often a lost cause. Soon my goal became to protect parents from feeling pressured so that together we could learn how to let their children lead us to their own readiness.

I thought it would be more effective to wait until the child showed signs of readiness for toilet training, and readiness to feel that it would be his own achievement. I began to work toward an approach of patience to offer parents. Many of them felt that they'd been traumatized by toilet training in their own childhoods and feared that they would repeat with their own children the pressured approach they'd experienced themselves.

I recorded the progress of 1,190 families in my practice who were willing to go along with my waiting-and-watching-for-the-child's-readiness scheme. (See Chapter 2 for this step-by-step approach to toilet training.) Together, we discovered that it really worked! Constipation was reduced to a minimum and bedwetting in children 5 years old and older dropped to an incidence of around 1 percent! Amazing.

When I published these results in *Pediatrics,* one of the journals most frequently read by pediatricians, this new, child-centered approach quickly took hold. Most pediatricians began to recommend a more sensitive approach, which meant waiting for the child's own mastery of toilet training challenges. Many of the symptoms I'd been so concerned about seemed to vanish in my own practice. Rarely did I have to prescribe treatment programs for smearing, severe constipation, soiling, and bedwetting. Putting the child's understanding that this achievement was his own before his parents' wishes for him to comply had naturally led to successful training and fewer problems later.

But there are still many obstacles and vulnerabilities that can threaten a child's success in this important developmental task:

1. A child may not be ready to face toilet training as soon as a parent is. With the pressures of nursery school or other caregivers, parents may find it hard to wait. Chapter 2 describes the signs of a child's readiness for toilet training, on which a parent might rely.
2. The temperament of the child can play an important role. A very quiet, sensitive child, for example, may need time to digest each step of toilet training, and decide when *he* is ready, before he will take it on. Children who are hypersensitive to touch will have to decide when they are ready to start sitting on an uncomfortably cold potty seat.

3. At the other end of the temperament spectrum, an active child at first won't sit still long enough for the potty. He may have to act out each step with a favorite toy, such as a dump truck, before he's ready to try it himself. Even then, he may sit still just to please others, not himself. A wise parent will watch for the child's cues of readiness and acceptance. Playacting the steps with toys and/or modeling clay may make it more understandable to the child. When he brightens and seems proud to have understood the meaning behind each step, it is time to leave it to him so he can feel this process is his to master.

4. Ghosts in parent's nurseries—for example, parents' bad memories of their own toilet training—are likely to make them anxious about their child's training. Many of the parents in my study were ready to admit that the fear of reproducing their own traumatic experience prevented them from introducing each step to the child without anxiety. I wish that all parents like this could recognize and accept their need for help to sort through their own past experiences. For such parents, it is all too easy to put on pressure, or to overreact—without meaning to—to a child's delay or failure in taking each step.

For many years after this study, a child-oriented approach to toilet training became widely accepted in this country. But as more parents of young children have had to go to work, as more children were started in childcare at earlier ages, pressure to toilet train children by a fixed, chronological deadline reemerged. Parents feel pressured by the requirement that their children be dry and clean for admission to childcare programs. (See "Preschool Pressure" in Chapter 3.) I think their children are responding to this pressure too: With these changes, I have noted a recurrent surge of delays in successful toilet training.

The *Children's Hospital Guide* from Children's Hospital Boston provides these more recent statistics on children's progress with toilet training between the ages of 2 and 5:

- 22 percent were out of diapers by age 2 and one-half years;
- 60 percent were out of diapers by age 3 years;
- 88 percent were out of diapers by age 3 and one-half;
- 20 percent were bedwetting up to age 5.

I'd be concerned whether this large number of 5-year-olds who wet the bed is evidence of the pressure that parents, and, in turn, children are feeling.

Specialized pediatric toilet training clinics are being set up for parents of 4-, 5-, and 6-year-olds who have not complied to toilet training pressure. An expert in pediatric urinary tract disorders at the Children's Clinic in Wilmington, Delaware, told me of his concern (and that of other pediatric specialists) about 3- and 4-year-old children who withhold urine as well as bowel movements. In extreme cases, the consequences of holding back on urine could be seen in X-rays of these children's enlarged ureters (tubes that carry urine from the kidneys to the bladder). Enlarged intestines in children who are holding back on bowel movements also seem, to me and to other pediatricians, to be on the rise again.

Parents are feeling the social pressures to get their children trained at an early age. These pressures are real. Often parents can't get their children accepted into childcare programs unless they are trained. Many involve institutional policy issues that cannot be solved by individual parents unless they band together. However, I would urge that we keep in mind the child's own role in his toilet training. This book offers a model intended to prevent problems such as these by focusing on the child's need to feel in control of his or her own body.

The remarkable thing to me is how thrilled a child can be when he does master this important step in his development. "Mommy, I'm dry! I'm clean!" What a triumph! Do we want to ignore that?

By 3 or 4 years, children face pressure from each other at preschool. One child is bound to ask another, "Are you dry at night?" The other nods his head vigorously, and asks, "You don't wear diapers?" "No!" the first child will emphatically answer. And yet, his bravado gives him away. Any sensitive adult watching this scene would know that the bragging child still wears diapers himself.

The pressure that children put on each other to be dry and clean is an important factor by the age of 4. We, as parents and professionals, had better not add to it, so we can support a child who is not ready yet. I hope this book can help parents be patient and understanding—and ready to admire a child as he works hard to make toilet training his own success, step by step.

CHAPTER **2**

The Touchpoints of Toilet Training

Preparing the Way

Before a child is ready for toilet training, she will first master a number of other abilities on which this new task will build. Her parents, too, will grow in their new role. Before they are ready for the job of toilet training their child, they will learn when to guide and when to stand back, and how to adapt to their child's unique personality. From the beginning of a child's life, the building blocks of toilet training are being assembled—for parents and child. At each opportunity for growth, the whole family is bound to falter as they ready themselves for the new step ahead. I call these opportunities "touchpoints."

During pregnancy, first-time parents-to-be have more important things to worry about than soggy diapers and smelly bowel movements. Though they may get the diapers, wipes, and changing table all set up ahead of time, sponging off that first sticky, green-black newborn stool (meconium) is hardly what they've been dreaming of. Experienced parents-to-be may even dig out newborn diapers leftover from their next oldest child, but they too are focused elsewhere, on *who* this new baby will be. Yet for many adults, cleaning up their baby's messy bottom, like losing sleep night after night to soothe and feed a wailing baby, is one of those selfless gestures that seems to transform them into a role they were not sure they could fill: They are parents!

The Newborn Touchpoint

When a new baby is born, parents inspect every inch—the face and wide-open eyes, of course, but also the fingers, the toes, the buttocks, and genitals. Hungry to get to know their new infant, their first questions are almost always: *Is it a boy or a girl?* (Even with prenatal ultrasounds, parents *always* are thrilled when they can finally see for themselves.) *Is she okay?* Parents also wonder: *How will I ever learn how to take care of my baby?* At the beginning they will want reassurance that their baby can feed and be soothed. For new parents, toilet training is a still distant test of this challenging role.

Over time, parents learn to feel confident in their ability to care for their child. Then they are ready to instill the same confidence in her: Modeling on her parents' confidence, she'll know that she can learn to care for herself too. Of course it is too early now to think of toilet training. But it is never too soon to think about the way the child experiences her body and her parents' caring for her body. These early experiences can help her learn later to enjoy taking care of herself, as she will in a few years when she decides she wants to "go potty like a big girl."

At first, though, the new responsibilities seem overwhelming. The first diaper change can be a harrowing experience. If they ever thought about it before the baby was here, parents might wonder, "How will I stand the filth and smell of it?" But now they have much more important questions: "Will I drop her? Have I wiped her clean enough yet? Her skin looks so fragile—what if she gets a rash? Will she ever forgive me for making her cry until she's red in the face?" Now, barely noticing how unattractive the baby's stools are, worries like these flood parents as they fall in love with their new baby. What a responsibility!

All of a young couple's passion centers on the baby's birth and delivery. She is glorious—a healthy, glowing newborn! But when they watch the nurses diaper their baby, they may panic. It looks so easy, but seems so hard on the baby.

When an experienced nurse lays a newborn on her back on the changing table, the baby may cry out, her little chin quivering. A busy nurse may ignore this. She deftly wipes off the baby's slightly soiled buttocks with a wet wipe, showing the parents how to wipe from front to back. She pulls the baby's legs up quickly and slips the fresh diaper under her. She quickly fixes the tapes around the diaper and in little more than a minute the baby is clean and diapered.

By this time a newborn may be crying loudly. It is all so sudden and intrusive. Her own startles—arms and legs flailing—make her cry all the more. At the nurse's suggestion, the mother may speak to her to calm her. When a baby hears her mother's already familiar voice, she may quiet abruptly.

When put to breast, if the baby is ready and not exhausted from the birth or medication, she may start to mouth and suck! As she roots about, she opens her mouth to latch on and pulls hard on the nipple. This may be quite a surprise for the mother, perhaps even painful.

As the parents watch this first feeding, they may get the next surprise. The baby may noisily produce a gurgling stream of blackened, sticky stool called meconium. This first bowel movement of life fills the diaper. The baby's legs are drawn up. Her face is red, her whole body tight and pushing, as if this process were painful.

"What to do? Clean her up? Calm her down? Continue to try to feed her?" All of these conflicting questions race through a new mother's head. The parents may call for the nurse or try to change her themselves. They remember the prenatal class lesson, "Never, never leave your baby on the changing table without a hand on her." Once they navigate this first adventure, the baby may begin to calm down. In between cries, she may catch the sound of her mother's voice, and her startling behavior may begin to smooth out. As she listens, her whole body seems to move in rhythm with her mother's voice. When parents offer soothing, but also help a child learn to soothe herself, they are setting up the earliest patterns for turning the learning back to the child. This is a step toward learning self-control that will be needed in toilet training later on.

The next challenge will be to help the baby learn to relax instead of startling when she's being changed. Then she can enjoy diaper changing as a time to be cared for.

Fathers who participate in diaper changes from the beginning also gain confidence in soothing the baby. When the baby responds, the rewards are enormous. Diaper changing becomes an expression of love between them. Who would have thought that one could fall in love over changing a diaper!

Each diaper change is an opportunity for this rewarding communication. It is the baby's chance to see her mother's face and to absorb her gentle approach, to see her father's face and take in his more energetic one. Over the next two months these become times for her to notice and remember these differences.

Parents become remarkably adept at the whole operation. Changing a baby, gently wiping her, watching her face respond, her whole body relax, gradually becomes an enjoyable time to play and communicate with the baby. The brief discomfort— for the parent, of dealing with the mess, and for the child, of the bladder or bowel contractions—becomes overshadowed by the anticipation of this chance to communicate. This early positive experience of diaper changes, then, is a first step toward making toilet training later on a pleasure, not a struggle.

2 Months

A new baby learns so rapidly to recognize and anticipate each parent as separate and important. By 6 to 8 weeks, research has shown that a baby can tell us—with her toes, fingers, mouth, and eyes—that she can distinguish a parent from a stranger leaning over to interact with her. In this short time, a small baby and her parents have learned to understand each other's signals and have established their expectations for communication. A small baby has already begun to store up what she knows about each parent's behavior. Unconsciously, parents will also be sopping up the baby's unique responses to each of them.

Parents' attitudes about their baby's body and diapering are bound to be expressed—and experienced by the baby—at each diapering interaction. These are early opportunities to set up positive patterns, important times for parent and child to learn about each other.

By 8 weeks, if parents lean over their baby to diaper her, every part of the baby's body begins to react with smooth movements. Facial behavior, toes, fingers, arms, legs all move in a rhythmic way—reaching out, pulling back, reaching out, pulling back in three to four cycles per minute. The face and eyes soften, then brighten, soften, then brighten—three to four times a minute. Clearly, she has learned to expect a rhythmic kind of interaction with her parents. She has learned to expect her mother to interact with her in a familiar and predictable way as she diapers her. The father will have a different style, often more playful, even joking. But this, too, will have become predictable for the baby.

When working parents ask me, as they always do: "Will she know me when I come home from work?" I can reassure them, "Watch for this behavior meant just for you. It will tell you how well she already knows what to expect from you."

The baby learns not only from the expectable repetition of each parent's unique approach, but from any subtle changes that occur at each of these times. She lets her parents know how special they are for her. They, in response, show her that: "You are important! You are special to me! I will listen and watch and respond to you in a way that fits with your own rhythms. We'll get locked in our game—every time I diaper you." If a parent continues to respect a child's cues, toilet training can become a time for communication too—though there will be new messages.

5 Months

By 5 months, the diapering game has changed. The baby will chortle. She will smile. She will reach out to grab your face as you lean over her. She may want to grab for a toy if you hold it up to her. Or she may already be twisting her body, to turn over. Her legs may bend to try to push her body. Few babies of this age still lie there passively while you reach for the washcloth, the ointment, the clean diaper. *Never* take your hand off her! At this age, a baby can easily roll off the changing table and fall to the floor—utterly devastating for both parent and baby.

Parents of an active baby have already become alerted to never leave her, but a quiet baby can surprise parents by her sudden mobility. Give your baby a toy to hold and explore with both hands, to mouth, to hold out at arm's length and examine, and to mouth again. She'll lie there long enough for you to clean her up, rub her with lotion, and diaper her!

Don't miss out on the opportunity to play again after it's all done. She'll still expect the reward of your face and voice. She'll still squiggle as you lean over her. She'll laugh out loud if you lean over to kiss her stomach. Blow on it! Growl into it! She'll scream with delight! She'll know that each diapering is a great game, a chance to let each other know how much in love you both are!

7–8 Months

By 7 or 8 months, a baby will be creeping on her stomach. She may still be going backward as she struggles unsuccessfully toward an object that has caught her eye. On her back, she has already learned how to increase the excitement of diapering. She'll arch up onto her legs and shoulders. She'll try to turn over. She'll show you how she's learned to move around in this position. As you lean over to diaper her, she'll be likely to squeal, and perhaps say "mama" or "dada" to get a response from you. If you turn away to reach for a new diaper, she may either become so active that you must keep a firmer hold, or may quiet as if to wait. Either way, hold on! She has learned the routine and may at times cooperate. Her face may even say, "Why don't you play with me? This is my time!"

If you give her a toy to try to distract her long enough to keep her quiet, she may comply by examining it carefully for a few moments. But then, she's likely to drop it overboard. She'll look up at you to see whether you'll retrieve it. If you do, she'll drop it again and again, laughing to see whether you'll play this new game. As you press her belly to hold her down long enough to clean her, she'll try all of her wriggles. If your baby is a boy, watch out! He is likely to pee all over everything. This can be quite a surprise for the baby as well as for you, since most of the time his genitals are hidden deep down in his diaper.

At the end of these new 7-month-old diaper games, be sure to keep playing the old ones—of smiling, of talking, of kissing your baby's stomach. They remind her of all the times she has enjoyed these diaperings. Stranger anxiety—when babies become more aware of other people, and then cling harder than ever to parents for reassurance—is peaking now. This new challenge is likely to give times for closeness a new importance—a way to refuel and get ready to take on the world!

10–12 Months

For a few months now, much of your baby's energy has been consumed by her need to move. Now, as her first birthday approaches, she can get away, and scare herself when she discovers she is "on her own." Diaper changes are another chance for her to wriggle away to play "catch-me-if-you-can!" She is so busy, so squirmy, that it takes a very determined hand to keep her on her back when it is time to change her diaper. A toy won't distract her for long enough anymore. She's learned that dropping it over the edge of the changing table is too much fun. As the toy disappears from view, she is testing out whether it is still anywhere at all, and whether it will come back. She is also testing you to see what will happen when you get exasperated!

By a year, a baby has learned to pull up, to stand. This new talent is so exciting that you may as well use it. Let the baby stand on the floor while you diaper her. Let her pull up and down on a railing or cruise on a safe piece of furniture while you change her. She'll be so ready to try her balancing act that she'll let you change her more readily if she can keep standing or moving the whole time. For messy diapers, you'll want to change her on the bathroom floor—or in the empty bathtub—as she pulls herself up and down and all along the bathtub. At least you can wash up more easily afterward. But don't let her bump her head on the faucets.

As you diaper your baby on her feet, tell her why you are doing it that way. "You are so great on your feet that I don't want to have to lay you down. You can help me change you already can't you?" By explaining what you are doing, you are letting her begin to understand and encouraging her to participate. This is an early opportunity to set up a pattern of cooperation to fall back on if future struggles emerge—as they may when it is time for toilet training. There are so many areas in which you cannot give her control. But she'll resent these less if you make it clear when she can be a "partner," with choices that can be left up to her. "When you want to lie down, we can play our old games." She may decide to do that, but she may not. Value this urge for independence.

As she approaches the end of her first year, a baby is already at work on three tasks that she will need later on, when she is ready for toilet training:

1. trying things out for herself and keeping you at bay;
2. finding out what happens to things when she can no longer see them; and
3. understanding what that look on your face means (for example, when you've had enough chasing and fetching), and how she ought to respond.

Once toilet training begins, she will want to handle her pee and BMs on her own, and keep you out of her business. She'll worry about what happens to her BMs as she watches them swirl down the toilet and out of sight. And she'll be checking your face to see if you're worried too, if you'll respect her as she masters the toilet for herself.

Too Soon for Toilet Training

At the 1-year-old pediatric visit, I ask every child's parents: "Have you thought about toilet training yet?"

Many parents look at me with surprise: "But she's only a baby. Isn't it too early to worry about that."

I agree: "I'm glad you think so too." But watch out! After her first birthday you may feel pressure. Your parents or other relatives may have been trained early themselves. They may even have tried to train you soon after the first year. They may tell you "Get going!" If they do, what will it mean to you?

Parents may answer, "Well, I guess it will make me feel guilty if I don't."

"That's why I want to warn you. You can say, 'Don't worry. We have a plan. I want to wait until she's ready. I have thought it over and I'll be ready when she is.'"

This leads us right into the next question: "What is the plan?"

"To wait until she is showing us signs of being ready to do it herself." I hope that by preparing parents in this way, they won't give in to pressure to push the child.

In many cultures, a parent's goal is to train the child in the first year by responding to her body signals with a race to the toilet, even though the child isn't yet aware that she needs to urinate or move her bowels. In southern Mexico, for example, Zinacanteco mothers I observed carried their babies on their backs all day—in a serape. They didn't put them down on the dirt floors to learn to crawl, to stand, and pull around. A mother was in constant touch with her baby. When she felt the baby's body getting ready to urinate or to have a stool, she became alert and responded. She was so sensitive to her that she could tell. She then held the baby away from her body and brought her outside the hut to urinate or to have a BM. When the baby began to walk in the second year, she was already conditioned to respect the inside of the hut. She toddled outside to try to urinate or defecate. Often, she wouldn't quite make it, but no one paid much attention. It was already up to her—and she knew what was expected.

I was amazed at the relaxed attitude of these Mayan people, and of their success in leaving it to the child. The close contact of mother and child was such a help, and there were no diapers to interfere with the mother's awareness of the child's body, and with the child's discovery of her own bodily sensations.

In our mainstream hygienic culture, we must find other ways of respecting the child's role in toilet training. There are critics of my child-centered approach, and of waiting until the end of the second year. They feel that parents in our culture could start earlier and be successful. They may often be right. But there is no way, in the first year, to know which children can succeed and which ones will not. Some children will not be ready for this early approach, and failures can feel humiliating to a child. Such failures—when children are pushed before they are ready to be successful—are likely to result in more serious problems such as withholding, smearing of bowel movements, or bedwetting later on.

My approach is based on being sure a child is ready, and allowing toilet training to be the child's success. As I mentioned, I came to this child-centered approach in response to the struggles of many children who were pressured to be trained before they were ready. But now parents, too, are under new pressures. Parents who feel pressure from important others on this issue are likely to pass this pressure on to the child. To protect children, parents need protection too. If the preparation I offer parents in this first year can help them withstand the feelings of being pushed to start earlier, then I have "touched" the family system at a first year "touchpoint."

18 Months

The excitement of walking, and of being independent, is so overwhelming to a child that this certainly is not a time for a parent to expect any interest in sitting still anywhere—especially on a toilet. Yet many parents come in for a checkup and say: "You were absolutely right about the pressure! My parents sent a potty seat in the mail." Or else: "The daycare center has already asked when I was going to start toilet training."

"How did it make you feel?" I ask.

"I felt as if I should get going."

"Can you wait until she's ready to take it over as her own step?"

Parents often reply: "If you say so, but I'd better be successful if I wait. What if I wait too long and miss the cues for when she's ready?"

"You won't. She'll let you know when she's ready."

"But I don't want her to go to college in diapers!"

"I don't either. And she won't. If you can wait until she seems ready, in my experience, she's less likely to fail."

Still not reassured, parents are bound to ask: "But, I hear so much about bedwetters and kids who won't go. What are we waiting for?"

I then lay out the seven early signs of readiness a child will show, and urge parents to wait for them. To me, these are the early skills the child will need if she's going to be successful and use the toilet the way others do, others around her whom she admires.

"That sounds like years away!"

"No, you won't have to wait until she is grown. I'm just suggesting that you wait for your child to take each of these steps first, so that she can feel successful when she cooperates."

Early Signs of Readiness

Sometime around her second birthday, a child may show some initial interest in the potty or training seat. But often this interest vanishes soon after, especially if eager parents have latched on with excitement. Don't be fooled by these early expressions of interest. Let these first steps be the child's.

Before 2 years of age, your child is *not* likely to be ready for toilet training. But it is time to begin to watch for seven new behaviors—usually not all present until after the second birthday—as the earliest signs of a child's readiness for toilet training. When one or two of these signs appear, parents are bound to want to forge ahead with toilet training. But the child is still not likely to be ready. Parents will need to wait for all seven to appear. Later on, there will be more advanced signs that a child is ready. These are the seven earliest signs of readiness:

1. *She's not as excited about walking and being on her feet all the time.* She's ready to sit down and learn a new task. She's made progress with walking, balancing, even running, and now is more interested in sitting still to learn to use her fingers for more complex activities. Most children are at least 18 months, often older, before this happens.

2. *She has receptive language,* that is, the ability to understand the words she hears, for example, a parent's wishes. Along with this, she can remember what she is told, and translate it into action. She can even listen to and carry out a two-step command: "Go to your bedroom and bring me a book for us to read together." And she's so proud of herself when she succeeds.

3. *She can say, "No!"* In other words, she needs the ability to make her own decision about whether she is ready or not. All too often a child may comply with toilet training for a period as if to please the parent. But then she may stop, as if she's realized "this wasn't *my* idea." She may even hold back her bowel movements and urine until she herself is ready. (If this leads to painful constipation, she'll have even more reason to hold back, setting up a vicious cycle.)

Don't push her before she knows how to tell you whether she's ready. Once she *can* protest with words when feeling the need to stand her ground, she will be able to make toilet training her own job.

4. *She will start putting things where they belong.* She may even begin to pick up her toys. She will put blocks in the box where they belong. She may even bring your slippers to you because she knows they belong with you, and not scattered across your bedroom floor! Some children this age not only begin to learn where things go, but also become very interested in arranging and organizing, for example, amusing themselves for long periods by carefully lining up toy cars or doll furniture. I am always amazed at this orderliness that crops up sometime after a child's second birthday. She is getting ready to use her potty as an appropriate place for her "products"—but not yet.

5. *She imitates your behavior.* A little boy walks like his father, and uses gestures like him. A little girl walks like her mother. She uses her hands to make gestures like her mother, or an older sister. As a toddler, she'll want her mother's shoes to wear. A boy puts his father's tie around his neck. This urge to imitate is a precious incentive for a child to want to use the toilet—"like mommy and daddy." Because children this age watch so closely to soak up and imitate their parents' behavior, outright pressure for them to use the potty or toilet is unnecessary. Children already know how grown-ups handle their pee and BMs, and they want so much to be just

like them. Trying to live up to their parents' behavior is already a daunting task. They are already pressuring themselves. Pressure from parents can make it seem hopeless.

6. *The child starts to urinate and move her bowels at predictable times.* As a child approaches 2 years of age, her urinary and digestive systems mature. She may begin to urinate and have bowel movements a little more predictably. She may remain dry for 1–2 hours at a time. Toward the end of this year, a child may even be dry throughout a nap. After a nap, it would be easy to "catch" her urine if she were rushed to a potty seat. Bowel movements may begin to occur at predictable times of the day—often during or just after a meal. These patterns are a real tease for waiting parents who may misunderstand them as a sign that the child is ready before she really is.

7. *She becomes aware of her body.* A child's awareness of her bodily functions often surfaces as she approaches 2 years of age. As she becomes more and more aware of her body, she'll begin pointing, noisily, to her wet diaper. She'll even grunt when she's trying to have a bowel movement. I urge a parent also to look for this sign: "Her awareness will be useful to help her train herself. She also needs to start labeling her body parts and functions with the words you'll use—poops, pee, bowel movements, penis, vagina, bottom, whatever. Your own words, or hers, are probably the best. All of these can be used to alert her to her bodily functions.

(Don't be surprised or shocked if a child begins to be aware of his or her sexual organs at times of diapering. Masturbating begins to surface when a boy has a chance to touch his penis, or a girl her vagina. Instead of reacting with surprise or embarrassment, be prepared to say "that's your vagina" or "that's your penis." Children have been covered up all these years and now they can be aware of these body parts, learn to name them, and understand some of their functions. A boy may get an erection at these uncovered times. These are also moments when you'll need to be prepared to dodge his spray.)

When I share these seven developmental steps with parents, they are likely to be only partially comforted: "But this may take forever!"

I assure them that these skills will come in a predictable way, and that toilet training will be much easier and more successful if they wait for them to appear.

2 Years

The child's job, or the parent's?: My wife was ready to get our third daughter out of diapers when she was 2½. I urged her: "Let her do it when she's ready." Our child overheard the conversation. I shall never forget her face when I came home every evening to see that she had saved her urine and stools in her potty to show me. She was so proud! And so was I—but I tried not to overdo my satisfaction and let it interfere with her feeling that she had conquered this step on her own. This was her victory, not mine.

Parents' impatience: During pediatric visits with parents in the second year, we reaffirm our goal, and watch and wait for signs of readiness. Together we can enjoy the earliest signs when they first emerge, and track them until they clearly say it's time to get started. But it can be hard for parents to wait. Most of the other touchpoints a child goes through leave parents with mixed feelings—excitement about the child's progress, and sadness about the passage of time and the baby left behind. Not so for toilet training. Parents are often ready for this step before the child is, and few are troubled by mixed feelings about leaving messy diapers in the past.

Of course parents are in a hurry. Diapers are expensive, and an environmental burden. Changing them is often messy and inconvenient. To this is added the pressure from the many childcare settings that require a child to be toilet trained for admission. Parents are also in a hurry because such a major accomplishment is hard to believe in until it has happened. Until the child has taken this major step, parents can't help but wonder "Will she ever take over?" "Will she be dating in diapers?"

In our mainstream culture, it has become a mark of success in parenting for a child to be successfully toilet trained. As with walking and talking, parents of young children often see early toilet training as a sign of intelligence, the sooner the more so. On the playground, parents ask: "Is your child out of diapers yet?" For some this question may call up feelings of anxiety or shame, and for others, pride. How important, how personal child rearing successes have become for parents in this culture! But when toilet training becomes a parent's pride, or shame, a child is bound to feel that her job has been taken out of her hands.

Pressure vs. Motivation: As the pressures on parents increase, their anxieties increase. This pressure, often increased by concern from relatives, is bound to be transmitted to the child. Of course parents can't entirely hide their increasing displeasure with messy diapers. Nor should they. A child needs the motivation to learn to use the potty that comes from her desire to please and to be like the adults, siblings, and toilet-trained peers she admires. Her sensitivity to her parents' wishes, her desire to be like them and to please them is all concentrated on this developmental step.

These expectations—from all corners—are so clear, and so powerful, that a child doesn't need *pressure* to be motivated to make this next step. Because a child wants so badly to succeed, to be "just like mommy, just like daddy," it is easy to see how parents' expectations can backfire when they turn into pressure. The 2-year-old does want to please. She does want to be a "big girl." She knows how to imitate her parents, and she wants to. But she needs to succeed at all of this as much for her own sake as for anyone else's. If she is to avoid being overwhelmed, she will need to know that it is up to her, and that she can proceed at her own pace. As a pediatrician, I try to be sensitive to the concerns of parents. At the same time, I want to alert them to the developmental issues in the child that can be harnessed to achieve success in this area, or that can throw it off course if disregarded.

In addition to the seven signs of readiness mentioned earlier, a 2-year-old will show other ways in which she is ready to start toilet training.

Ready to Say Goodbye—to Poop: A child of 2 will have developed what we call "object permanence." She can walk away from her parents and watch them "disappear" around a corner while knowing that they should still be there. She knows she can keep her parents in her mind even when she can't see them. But this new ability means that she will be concerned about disappearances, and it can be shaky at times of separation.

This is the age at which some children watch intently as the water drains out of the bathtub, worried about where it goes, whether they might get sucked down too. Some children even wonder what might come back up out of the bathtub or toilet drain! Think of how confusing it must be to a 2-year-old to watch her poop swirl down the toilet drain to disappear forever: "Where does it go? Will it ever come back again? Is it still somewhere, even if I can't see it?" It's no wonder that she may hesitate, or even want to hold onto her poop. She must come to feel ready—to let go of her poops, and to picture in her mind that what seems to her to be a precious part of herself is still somewhere.

A Time for Testing: This is the age when children test parents with negativity. Temper tantrums are the peak. In these episodes, as they struggle over issues that no one cares about but them, they are testing their own and their parents' limits. "Can I let myself give in, or not? I must test them until I know for myself." The 2-year-old watches parents' faces, and their body language, very carefully. She is learning about them, but also about herself. She needs to know that they will set the limits that she needs, even when she protests. But she also needs to know that her parents are still available to her, even after a screaming meltdown, to soothe her, to help her learn to soothe herself, to reassure her that one day she will get these blow-ups under control.

It is easy to see how premature efforts to toilet train a 2-year-old can get caught up in these battles. Two is the worst time of all for such skirmishes. The danger is that toilet training can become another battleground for testing limits and tantrums, rather than an opportunity for the child to experience control over herself and her body. A parent would do far better to pick battles carefully, set limits that can be enforced, and protect important areas such as toilet training from becoming war zones. Because toilet training is not a limit that parents can enforce, it must be left up to the child.

The second year is called "the terrible twos." But it should be labeled "the terrific twos." Think how much she is learning, about herself, about her limits, about her world. Why, indeed, should a 2-year-old give in passively to a parent's wish when she can learn so much more by testing them and herself? Toilet training needs to be kept out of these struggles. Parents can help if they let the child know that they know it's her job.

New Rituals and Signs of Readiness: Diapering sessions are opportunities for parent and child to be close again, a closeness needed now as the cement for a relationship stressed by the 2-year-old's testing. Why, indeed, would a 2-year-old want to give up these close times for a cold potty? Many children are helped to make the transition from diapers to potty with the reassurance that this can still be a chance to be together. Offer to read her a story, sing songs together, or chat together as the child sits on the potty (while you perhaps are enthroned on your "grown-up potty").

The following signs of readiness will let parents "know" when the child is ready to start. Parents are likely to notice these after a child turns 2:

More Signs of Readiness

Toilet talk:

Toward the end of the second year, a child will begin to announce—often with excitement and pride, "I peed!" Or "I went poop, mommy." She may even pull at her wet or dirty diapers as if she wanted to be changed.

Toilet play:

At 2, a child's fantasy play can help her try out and master questions and fears about her bodily "productions." She can put her doll or truck on the potty "to go pee like mommy." At the end of the second year, she uses fantasy to reproduce what

(continued on next page)

More Signs of Readiness
(continued from previous page)

she sees around her—she's been watching closely, and taking it all in. This sign of readiness may be the most important in timing the introduction of the toilet.

Getting dressed, and undressed— "all by myself":
A 2-year-old can pull on her socks. She can pull up her shirt. She can pull down her pants, and—toward the end of the second year—put them on. She will be becoming aware of her body, and of the independence of dressing and undressing herself.

Awareness of how other people use the potty:
Two-year-olds are ready and working hard to find out as much as they can about what other people do. This is an important way for a child to learn about using the toilet. I remember the noise of tiny rushing feet to see what I was doing whenever I made any noise urinating. "I'm going to my potty. Someday when you want to, you'll go to yours. You'll be such a big girl." But don't set up the potty as a requirement, or she'll be more likely to rebel against it later.

Increased imitation:
Though imitation begins earlier, a 2-year-old's imitations become even more exciting and complex. Imitation becomes almost a fetish. Now, not only will a little girl copy her mother's gestures and a little boy strut in imitation of his father, but each will imitate older siblings and friends. Watch two 2-year-olds play together. One will imitate a whole sequence of the other child's behavior without even appearing to watch him. Imitation is at a peak at the age of 2. Often a second or third child needs little training. She'll imitate her siblings.

If parents can wait through the second year, it is so easy to use these developmental steps to introduce the potty. Parents have often come to me as several of these signs begin to appear. "She's so aware of when she urinates and moves her bowels. Why shouldn't I start now?" And sure enough, at 18 months old, I can watch this child point to her diaper as she urinates into it in my waiting room. In my waiting room, she grunts as she has a bowel movement. But, as she does so, she hides in the corner. This is an important clue—although she is just beginning to learn, she isn't ready to share her learning with us. I encourage parents of children at this early stage to hold out for more signs of readiness to pile up, such as wanting to imitate, wanting to put things in their proper containers.

When a parent can't wait and puts the toddler on the pot "to catch her and show her what we want from her," the child may allow herself to be caught. But watch her face. A stony look will spread over it. She will look at you with flat eyes as you rush her to the toilet. Her arms may hang loose, her feet and legs stiff. She is trying to say: "I'm not ready yet." A parent will do best to respect these cues. She is showing you the cost to her of having an important step taken way from her.

Toilet Training: Step by Step

It is easier to keep toilet training a shared process, between parent and child, when it is taken one step at a time. Each step is intro-

Signs That a Child Is Not Ready

A child is not ready if she:

1. stands at the potty and then pees on the floor.
2. doesn't want her diaper taken off at all, screaming and struggling when a parent tries.
3. takes off her diaper and then has a bowel movement on the floor.
4. struts around with a broad gait, and then sits down with a mushy stool in her diaper. She appears not uncomfortable, but blissful.
5. goes off to hide in a corner or a closet where she can be heard grunting as she has a bowel movement.
6. says "no, no, no" if a parent comments that she seems to be ready for a bowel movement.
7. shows any resistance whatsoever to using the potty or toilet.

duced when the child is interested. If negativism, which is near the surface at 2, hits at any point along the way, immediately pull back to the preceding step. You may even need to start back at the beginning again. Reassure yourself: "When she's ready again, we'll start all over. I'll watch her for signs of accepting the step, and readiness for the next one." In this way, you can let her lead you. She may understand the idea of toilet training, but don't confuse this with her readiness to go along with it. This way you'll be less likely to hit a brick wall—of refusal or withholding.

If your child senses your eagerness, she may feel that you will take her triumph-to-come away from her. Then she's bound to shut down. Your child may not even be aware of her negative response to your eagerness. You might say, "How does she know I'm eager?" Ask yourself how she knows you mean it whenever you tell her to "stop!" She knows the difference between: a commanding tone, and an expression on your face that matches your voice on one hand and, on the other, a casual tone and expression that says "Please don't, dear." She knows the difference immediately. Her sensitivity to you is great. Can you match it with your own sensitivity to her?

You will certainly need to be sensitive to your child's cues to work on toilet training with her. For this is a task over which she needs control. It will demand that she be ready to contain herself, and to go to a place that you specify. To perform for you demands an enormous amount of compliance. She can't help but feel a twinge of distress if she loses her own control. Be prepared to let her lead you—but you must really mean it!

Step 1—When she's ready for her own potty, take her with you to pick one out. She'll need a potty that sits on the floor—one that's hers, that she can pull around the house (preferably when it's empty!), one to try her favorite doll or stuffed animal on when she begins to understand your wish. Talk about it: "That one's yours. This is mine and daddy's (or mommy's). But you have your own and someday you'll use it like we do." Don't use deflectors (plastic shields that are meant to direct a boy's urine stream into the potty) for little boys' potties. Sooner or later, he is likely to sit down on it and hurt himself. Then, he won't sit on the potty again.

(A boy who learns to pee in his potty will take so much pleasure in the noise it makes that he'll learn quickly how to hold his penis down so he can spray the sides of the pot. Or, he will want to stand and to spray the room. Don't start him standing up. If you do, he'll never learn to sit down! He'll have far too much fun trying out his aim, inside the potty and out.)

Step 2—If the child shows any interest in her new potty, let her sit on it in her diapers, or fully clothed, while you sit on "yours." A cold potty seat is too big a step. Only sit her there as long as she's interested. Read her a story, or make one up, or sing to her. When she wants to run off, let her. You are simply introducing the routine—once a day. It's too soon to have her sit down on the potty undressed. Don't try to "catch" her yet when she's ready to urinate or move her bowels.

Step 3—Once she's gotten used to the routine of sitting while you sit, and of communicating together as you both sit, take her to the bathroom to undo her diaper and empty it into the potty. She may resist. One of my child patients said to her mother: "That's my potty. Don't you get it dirty!" If your child does not want to empty her diaper into the potty, pull back. But if she's willing, take her once or twice a day after she's wet or dirty to dump the diaper contents into her potty to help make the connection. She may even let you know when it's time for your bathroom trips. She may say, "Go to potty" when she's wet or dirty. You might want to start hand washing afterward as a routine. Get her a stool to stand on. Let her wash her hands "like you do." Watch her face to see whether she's getting interested and involved in these routines.

Step 4—is a big step. Offer to take off her diaper and to let her run around bare-bottomed. Put the potty in her room (or out in the yard with her if you have access to one; if there are neighbors nearby, some parents may be more comfortable covering the child with pull-up bottoms). Ask her whether she'd like you to help her "go potty" herself. Amazingly, she may have gotten the idea. And she may even be ready to use it! If she is, don't go overboard. Let her know in a calm voice that that was what you had in mind. "You went potty just like mommy and daddy do." But be calm, no matter how thrilled you are. If you get too excited you'll overwhelm her. And in the process, you may be interfering with her chance to be proud of herself.

Step 5—If she is really involved in her success, rather than just trying to get you excited each day, offer her training pants that she can pull up and pull down by herself. Then, she'll be on her way!

When the child is interested, you can offer her the chance to plop her bowel movement out of the potty and into the big toilet. Otherwise don't dispose of it until she loses interest.

When the child is interested, you can let her flush it herself.

When the child is interested, you can get her a stool or step to climb up to the big toilet to sit on it "like mommy, like daddy, like brother." But it may be wise to seat her backward, facing in. This gives her a chance to watch her pee come out of her body and sprinkle into the toilet water—a fascinating event for any child this age. Or use a potty seat that adapts to the big toilet seat to make it smaller, and safe. Too often children slip and feel like they're falling into the toilet. This is frightening! It's bound to put off another try for a long time. Seating a boy backward on the toilet seat might save the bathroom floor. But I'd advise that you be prepared for messes around the toilet anyway while a boy is learning the joys of spraying the world.

When a boy is interested, after learning to use the potty sitting down, he can learn to stand "like daddy, or big brother."

When a child is interested, try training pants at nap time, but don't be surprised if she's wet afterward. Don't let her feel defeated. Go back to diapers quickly. If you can be confident that this is only a temporary delay, you'll be able to offer her the reassurance and encouragement she'll need. (See "Dry at Night" in the next section.)

3–5 Years

By 3, many children will have mastered toilet training and be ready to move on to new challenges and victories. Some will not, and will need more time. (See Chapter 3, "Problems and

Solutions," for information on when a parent should be concerned.) But in either case, new demands and pressures can temporarily throw a child off course.

Touchpoints—a step forward, a step back: After any family stress, such as a move, a parent's absence, or a new baby, expect your child to fall back a few steps. This also often happens as a child faces a touchpoint, a demanding new developmental advance. You need not feel defeated when your toilet-trained child suddenly wets or soils again. But you'll want to watch for signs of your child's discouragement. Help her to understand the pressure and to see her reaction as acceptable: "You know, it's not easy having Mommy away," or "A new baby is a big change for all of us. Of course you need diapers again right now. Don't worry. It won't be long before you'll be back in training pants and can take over again. Lots of kids need to start over after something like this happens."

Any big event in the family can bring a regression in toilet training. Any step a child must make, such as going to a new preschool, or going away with the family, or accepting a new baby will do it. Any new fear (as is common at 4 or 5—see our book *Touchpoints Three to Six*) is likely to set her backward. If she feels that she has failed in your eyes for any reason, this may also be enough to cause a temporary backward slide. If she becomes ill, she may also lose recently gained ground.

You may need to reassure the child over and over, but follow her lead carefully. Her self-esteem is at stake. Being toilet trained is like any other step in development. If she can do it for herself, it will be a boost to her self-confidence. If she's doing it for you, or if she feels like she's failing, and disappointing you, her positive feelings about herself may be in danger. No achievement is worth that price. When she's ready to try staying dry again, she can start first with daytime, and then naptime. After she's proven to herself that she no longer needs a diaper for her nap, you can offer to help her stay dry at night. This challenge is the most difficult of all. Encourage her to readjust her expectations for this new task: "You may have a few accidents, especially at first, but you'll get there." Be sure she's ready for this step, so that you can be sure you haven't set her up to fail.

Dry at Night: One of my own children was slow in learning to stay dry at night. As I was changing his sheets with him one morning, he surprised me:

"Why do you care so much, Daddy?"

"I don't," I answered emphatically.

Without batting an eyelash he replied, "Yes, you do."

Not only was he right, but after setting me straight in this way he never wet the bed again! I had been completely unaware of how much his struggle mattered to me, and how much my pressure mattered to him.

Why do we care so much that we add our own pressure to theirs? I have heard a 4-year-old say: "I'll never be dry at night." What discouragement! Up to 20 percent of children may still be wetting at night at age 5. Such children needn't feel that it's a serious failure. Unfortunately, they often do.

Staying Dry at Night

- Don't start until she's ready and asks to "be dry at night."
- Don't start too early. If you do, she'll be discouraged when she fails, and will be reluctant to try again.
- Wait until she's been dry during naps.
- Wait until she's able to go without using the potty or toilet for prolonged periods (3–4 hours) during the day.
- Keep her in diapers or heavy pull-ups until you are pretty sure she'll make it. Even then, go back to them if she fails.
- Don't ever shame her.
- Don't act too excited when she is dry after a nap, or when she wakes up dry in the morning. Once again, it's got to be *her* achievement, not yours.
- Offer to put a potty by the side of the bed at night. Buy a special one. Paint it with luminous paint. Call it her own "night-time potty."
- Get her up before you go to bed. Be sure she's really awake. Carrying a sleeping child to a potty to empty her bladder doesn't provide the learning she will need to get up to go at night on her own.
- Use a rubber sheet under the sheet so urine won't wet the mattress. This way it will matter less if she's wet.
- Limit after-supper drinks—the less the better. But try not to make it an issue. If you do, she'll feel cheated, or stressed. Neither will contribute to her cooperation.
- Encourage the child to try to wait a little longer in the daytime before urinating, *if she's interested.* If she can hold on to her urine a little longer, this will help increase her bladder control. She can also try to stop and start her urine to strengthen her sphincter (the muscles that open and close the bladder) control.

(See "Bedwetting" in Chapter 3.)

Holding Back Bowel Movements: Sometimes during this period a child may start holding back on her bowel movements, hiding in a corner when she must go. She's letting you know how private she needs her bodily functions to be.

Many children want to be "left alone," with the freedom a diaper gives to perform when and where they want. Let the child know that you understand. "We can go back to diapers or to pull-ups. You decide. Don't worry about it." Be sure not to add your discouragement to hers. If your child is holding back her bowel movements, talk with your pediatrician about starting her on a stool softener so her bowel movements won't be hard enough to hurt her. An early start with this gentle medicine—when needed—can prevent more aggressive measures such as mineral oil, laxatives, suppositories, or enemas later. Once her stools do become painfully hard, she's bound to become scared of moving her bowels, and she will hold back all the more. (See also "Constipation, Soiling, Megacolon" in Chapter 3.)

Accident in the Bathtub: Parents can be horrified by this rather common event. The calmer you can be the better. Extract the bowel movement from the water, if you can. A strainer or aquarium-size fishing net may help. (Be sure to wash it thoroughly afterward.) Change the water after she's through pooping. Fortunately, a child's immunity to the bacteria of her stool is pretty effective. If you get too excited, your reaction is bound to encourage her to repeat the performance. As she becomes more interested in the potty, you can put the potty seat in the tub, to see if she can catch her poop in the pot. This may help her make the association as to where poops are eventually meant to go.

Playing Fireman: A boy just beginning to discover how he can spray his urine is bound to experiment. Is it warm and private enough in your backyard for you to let him play out there without his diaper or clothes on? Let him know that the living room is not the place for this, but he can try it outside. If not, try the bathtub. If he gets a big reaction out of you when he experiments, he's bound to try it again as a way of getting you involved. Surprise him with your undivided attention at other times when he's not expecting it or asking for it. This will balance your attempts to restrict where he pees.

Too Late for the Toilet: Sometimes children have accidents when they have been so enthralled with their play that they "forget" they have to go to the bathroom—until it's too late. By the time they make it there, there just isn't time to unsnap, unzip, and get in position. See if she'll agree to let you give her gentle reminders ("Do you need to use the bathroom?") periodically. But don't overdo it—it's pressure! This is a more preventive measure than anything you can do after the fact, and it will teach her to pay more attention to her bladder on her own. Also, be sure her clothing is easy to get off and on. Belts are sure to slow a little boy down, and the straps of overalls are hard to undo unless they can be slid over the shoulders.

It is common for children at this age to lose ground in an area where they have previously made a major accomplishment. Sometimes the backsliding is the price a child pays for a new step about to be taken—a touchpoint. Be on the lookout for a new challenge your child has taken on.

When a Child Holds Back on Bowel Movements

Watch her face and gestures to understand what she is trying to say, and when she is ready to try the potty again:

- Don't ever give up hope, or begin to push her.
- Don't ever punish her for failures.
- Don't let others interfere with your routine.
- Don't clean her up or flush her bowel movement away until she's ready.
- Get help (such as a stool softener) early from your doctor or nurse to prevent your child from becoming frightened of her own hard and painful bowel movements.

Such backsliding can make a child anxious. She may become easily discouraged or feel guilty. She may even fear that she'll never grow up, that she'll never please you again. Reassure her that setbacks like these happen to everyone and that they aren't as serious or discouraging as they may seem.

Setbacks at School: If your child is in daycare, discuss with her teacher the routine (for example, avoiding pressure, using diapers when she feels the need, etc.) you and your child have established to deal with this temporary step backward. If the teacher can support her in carrying out your routines, you'll avoid confusing her. Otherwise, she's bound to have trouble figuring out how to please both of you. Of course you, as her parent, are always more important to her and to her self-esteem.

But when she's feeling discouraged, she'll need approval from all of the important adults in her life.

Teachers, understandably, will want to get the child trained—again—in a hurry. They may exert more pressure than they are aware of. Renewed bedwetting or holding back on bowel movements is a sign that you and the teacher will need to talk things over together. The child may comply at school, but save up her bowel movements and even her urine to regress and wet at home. Let her. Understand it and help her to understand it: "You are trying so hard to please your teacher that you just can't expect to manage at home too. I won't expect it right now either. You are trying so hard." Be sure you don't push her at home. If you do push or scold her at home, you'll need to find the courage to apologize: "I'm sorry I was in such a hurry. You don't need to worry. You can take your time. I do understand now."

A 3-year-old and her mother came in to see me because the child—recently toilet trained—had started wetting and soiling again. The mother told me: "She just won't use the potty. I know she knows what she's doing. She used to use it." As I started to reply, she started to ask her child to wait in my waiting room. She said, "I don't want to talk in front of her." I replied, "No. This is her business and I want her to know what I'm going to say. She already knows how much it upsets you." Meanwhile, the little girl was playing with the dollhouse in my office as if she weren't paying any attention to us. I continued: "It's got to be up to her. Let her slip back a little. Put her in diapers or training pants and don't push her. And you may not like this idea, but I think it will help her a lot if you can apologize for pushing her." The mother seemed to agree, but I wasn't sure.

The next day, the same mother called me: "Do you know that when I went to put her on the pot, she said to me, 'Dr. B said to leave me alone. It's *my* potty!' She had listened to every word." I replied, "If you can leave it up to her, she'll decide when she's ready again. Now, apologize to her and you'll have it made. After that, don't say a word about it again." Later, this mother told me that her 3-year-old had nodded brightly to her apology. After a week, during which the mother said nothing further about toilet training, the child was using the potty again.

Your child needs your support and your understanding. Each developmental step—as important as this one to everyone in a child's life—is bound to cost the child a certain amount. Be grateful that she can and will save any regression for you, as the safest and most important person to understand, to accept, and, later, to help.

CHAPTER 3

Toilet Training Problems and Solutions

Accidents

(See also "Bedwetting," "Constipation, Soiling, Megacolon" "Diarrhea," and "Urinary Tract Infections.")

Accidents happen. They often occur when a child is under pressure or is making an adjustment to a new demand. But they can occur when a child is having a coughing fit, or when he has to hold out too long. He may even wet when he's giggling. It is common for a child to be so excited about playing that he fails to pay attention to his bladder's signals. He will squirm, wriggle, and maybe even hold himself. Parents will know he's doing the "pee-pee" dance—even if he doesn't. At times like these, all he needs is a gentle reminder: "Do you need to go pee? You can come back and play some more as soon as you're done." In general, though, parents' reactions to accidents should be kept to a minimum. The less attention the better.

The child is likely to take accidental wetting or soiling more seriously than they deserve. Watch his face—Does he look sad or worried? Does his head hang? These are signs that he is taking the accident too seriously. Let him know you understand. You can help him understand why he may have had an accident. "You have just gotten used to being out of diapers. Of course, you're likely to make mistakes. Particularly after you've had a big fight with your older brother, or if mommy is going away. (A parent can mention any unusual pressure on the child.) I get tense too, and then I make mistakes. Don't worry about an accident like this. It's not the end of the world. You can control yourself most of the time. You've worked so hard and I hate to see you discouraged."

If he's really preoccupied about this, there may be something more serious on his mind. Don't probe, but do watch for it. Listen for it. Perhaps you'll hear: "They called me spoiled at school, and teased me about being a baby."

A common reason for accidents is a new baby in the house. After the initial adjustment has been made, and everyone assumes it's over, a recently toilet-trained child may start wetting again. The baby may have just made a new step in development—like crawling or standing. This is such an exciting step for the whole family that their attention may set in motion the older child's sibling rivalry. Wetting again may be a symptom of this new stress he feels.

Rather than being upset with the older child, try to understand it and to share it with him. Let him fall back on diapers
or training pants until he is ready to try again. Unconsciously,
he may be imitating the baby, but that would be too much to
expect him to understand and to face. You might say, "You
know, most kids need to go back to diapers for a little while
every now and then. Don't worry. It won't be for long. You'll
want to grow out of them again soon. I'm not in a hurry and I
hope you're not. When I change you, you can be my baby
again, too."

If the accidents happen frequently in a child who has been
trained for awhile, there might be a medical cause. Parents will
then want to consult the child's doctor. For instance, when a
child (particularly a girl) starts wetting repeatedly after she's
been dry for several months, she should be checked by her doctor for a urinary tract infection.

Bedwetting (Nocturnal Enuresis)

Of all the toilet training steps, staying dry at night is the most
difficult. Don't expect it to come until well after your child learns
to use the toilet during the day. For a child to hold onto urine all
night demands a number of accomplishments, including:

- The child's bladder, sphincters (the muscles that keep the
  bladder shut), and the rest of his urinary tract must be

sufficiently mature, as well as the hormones that influence the production of urine;

- Sleep cycles also need to be developed enough so that the sensation of a full bladder can rouse him from deep sleep to a wakeful state.

For many children who still wet the bed, these have not yet matured. Their pace needs to be respected.

When to Worry: According to the Children's Hospital Boston *Guide* (see Appendix), 12–20 percent of 5-year-olds and 8 percent of 6-year-olds aren't able to stay dry all night. By 6 years of age it is certainly worth bringing this to the attention of your pediatrician. He or she will first check to be sure that there are no medical causes or major stresses related to the bedwetting. Be sure to get help at the earliest sign that a child's self-image might be in jeopardy—or before. When a child begins to restrict his activities, refusing to sleep at a friend's house, or appears evasive or ashamed about his bed's damp sheets, it is surely time to look for help.

Bedwetting in a Previously Dry Child: It is helpful to distinguish between bedwetting that starts up in a child who has been dry for at least 6 months from that of a child who has not yet stayed dry at night. If a child has been dry for at least 6 months and then begins to wet again repeatedly (often enough for it to be a nuisance), it is important to consider several possible reasons. Most of the time there has been a change, a disruption, or stress—sometimes mild, for example, a family trip, a minor illness, a parent out of town for work, a change in routine, or an exciting new event, sometimes major (a move, or a new baby in the family), sometimes more serious (see below). Bedwetting can also occur when a child is about to take a new developmental step ahead, a time when you can expect a temporary step backward in another area—a touchpoint.

Only a minority of children who wet their beds after age 5 (roughly 10 percent) will have a medical explanation for their renewed bedwetting. Be sure the doctor tests your child's urine. Does the child have a burning sensation on urinating? Children who have urinary tract infections (more likely in girls) may also be urinating more than usual. Girls this age with urinary tract infections may need to be reminded to wipe themselves from front to back so that they do not introduce bacteria that can cause infection from their feces into their urinary tract. Juvenile diabetes is another cause. The first symptoms may be frequent urination, increased drinking and eating, without weight gain, and then weight loss. Very rare causes of new, repeated bedwetting include neurological disorders.

Bedwetting in a child who has been dry can also be triggered by distressing events in the child's life: for example, the death or serious illness of a close family member, severe strain in the parents' relationship, or a divorce. Sexual molestation is an uncommon cause of bedwetting in a child who had previously been dry, but also needs to be considered when repeated bedwetting suddenly emerges—as if out of the blue. If this is a concern, your pediatrician should refer you to mental health professionals experienced in making this assessment. If confirmed, psychological help is of course needed.

If the child's pediatrician can find no medical cause, try to identify a stress that may have precipitated this symptom. Share it with the child, so he can understand the reason for his set-back or "failure" (as he will see it). Of course you may feel disappointed and he's likely to sense it—and he will be disappointed in himself. If you do get angry or exasperated, apologize to him. Try saying, "I know you don't like it either. We'll work on it together. If I can help you, I will, but I want you to tell me to lay off when it feels like I'm pushing you."

Persistent Bedwetting—Possible Causes: When a 6-year-old has never been consistently dry at night, his pediatrician will probably want to look for some of the causes described above. But when it has remained a problem until this age, it is even more likely that the bedwetting is the result of an immature urinary system or sleep pattern. Here are some examples of the usual temporary delays that are thought to cause persistent bedwetting:

- A small bladder, or a normal-sized one that can't hold onto urine when full.
- Decreased antidiuretic hormone (ADH), a chemical the body makes to control urine production. Sometimes, a synthetic form of this hormone (DDAVP) can be prescribed by his pediatrician, though usually this is best saved for short-term use—like sleepovers and summer camp.
- Difficulty in arousing from deep sleep at night—an immature sleep pattern in which sleep cycles don't rouse him to urinate. Insufficient sleep may make this worse.

What It Means to Parents: Of course a child's bedwetting is a burden for parents: more sheets and pajamas to wash, disrupted sleep and fatigue when the child wakes up after wetting the bed, and worries about what the bedwetting means, and whether it will ever end. Sometimes the harder parents try to help the worse the bedwetting gets—especially when the child is not ready to participate. Then, frustration adds to a parent's load. But there may be some relief in knowing that the child who wets the bed does not do so on purpose, and that he will participate when he is ready. It may also be reassuring for parents to know that the majority of such children—whose urinary tracts are developing more slowly—will eventually master this challenge, without treatment.

"Ghosts from the Nursery": A child's bedwetting can have other important meanings for parents when parents themselves were "bedwetters" as children. They are likely to relive their own struggle through their child's, and feel an even more desperate urgency to make the bedwetting stop, even if the child is not yet ready. Parents with bedwetting in their pasts are very likely to have children who wet the bed: Roughly 40 percent of children wet the bed if one parent had the same problem as a child; 75 percent of children with two parents who wet the bed will do so. It may be that the parents' own painful memories make it difficult for them to relax and wait. In any event, bedwetting need not be considered a problem, unless the child has come to see it as one. Sooner or later, it does clear up.

What It Means to the Child: Even when help is needed, and sought, it is important for parents to avoid emphasizing the bedwetting as a major concern—it already is for the child, even if he acts as if it weren't. It has probably already become a threat to his self-esteem. Honor his feelings about this, but don't add to them.

A 6-year-old might be heard to say, "No one else my age wets the bed. I can't sleep over at my friend's house. If he found out I still wet the bed he'd tease me for being a baby. Kids started teasing me about bedwetting when I was in nursery school. I said they were wrong. But they were right. Will I ever stop wetting the bed?" A child's discouragement and sense of hopelessness can certainly damage his self-esteem. Helping the child handle these feelings should be parents' main focus.

What To Do: Wait until the child has demonstrated a readiness to be dry all night. That means he's dry at naps. He's eager to be in pull-up pants. He wants your help to stay dry. The longer he's in diapers until he's really ready the more sleep you will all get. There is no advantage in starting too soon. Pressure on a child to stay dry early may increase the risk of bedwetting later on. In a child who is already bedwetting, pressure can often cause more bedwetting, and it certainly can affect the child's self-image.

"Bladder Power" Exercises: Encourage your child to practice these exercises during the day to help strengthen his bladder and sphincter muscles to work better at night:

- When he feels the need to urinate, ask him to try holding back his urine for a few minutes;
- When he starts to urinate, ask him to practice starting and stopping his stream;
- Have him practice getting up to go to his nighttime potty.

Helping Your Child Overcome Bedwetting

- Cover his mattress with plastic.
- Be ready for a nighttime accident so that you can make the cleanup easy and uneventful in the morning.
- Let him sleep on a towel he can remove if he wets.
- Give him a change of nightclothes to put on himself if he needs to.
- Leave a plastic hamper with a tight cover in his room where he can put wet sheets, towels, and pajamas.
- Offer to buy him a special nighttime potty that you and he can paint with luminous paint. Put it by his bed "to use at night."
- Set up a routine of emptying his bladder before he goes to sleep. Maybe he could use his nighttime potty for this.
- Use a nightlight.
- Suggest that you can get him up before you go to bed at night, if he agrees. (Some pediatricians recommend against this. But if it is offered supportively rather than punitively, I have found such nighttime waking to help reduce accidents later on in the night.)
- When you do, be sure he's awake and crawls out of bed *on his own* ("Remember, you wanted me to help you") to go to his night potty. But be sure he gets enough sleep.
- If the above steps are not working, put the child back in diapers, or into pull-ups. It may embarrass him to go back into diapers. But you are trying to let him get the feeling of a dry bed in the morning, so that he will be less likely to get used to a wet one. This may help him learn to begin to rouse when he starts to wet himself. Being well rested may too.
- Limit beverages from suppertime on, but don't make a big deal of it. Be sure to avoid soda drinks with caffeine, as they stimulate urination.

Once your child understands how to do these exercises, let him practice them on his own, so that he knows that this is his job not yours. Don't bother with them at all if he puts up a fight.

Medication: His doctor can prescribe medicines, such as DDAVP, a nasal spray that supplements a natural hormone that reduces the amount of urine produced. This works only in some children, and his bedwetting will be likely to return when the drug is discontinued. It is usually prescribed only on a short-term basis, for example, when a child is invited on a sleepover, or to help a child stay dry while away at overnight camp. This medication should be used only under the guidance of the child's physician, and with the child's consent. Be sure he feels that he is participating in his own treatment. If you warn him beforehand that it doesn't always work, he'll feel less discouraged if it doesn't help. If it does, you want him to feel that it is his own achievement.

Bedwetting Alarms: With an older, discouraged child who is desperate for help, a bedwetting alarm may be a solution. It is an alarm that attaches to his bedclothes and awakens him when he starts to wet. Even if he is motivated to get up to urinate, it can still take several months before the child is able to master this by himself. Don't bother with it if he isn't interested. It can all too easily feel like a punishment unless it is used sensitively. The risk is that the alarm may seem to say to the child: "You can't do it yourself, so I have to do it to you." Each alarm then becomes a reminder of his own inadequacy.

Being dry at night is a major step for the child and for the parents. But too much pressure to achieve this can make the child

What Not To Do When a Child Wets the Bed

1. Never discuss the child's bedwetting with anyone without the child's permission: "Can you let the doctor know you want to work on this? Or would you like me to?"
2. Never discuss the child's bedwetting in public. But don't make it a big secret either. Siblings are bound to know. Within the family, it is best discussed in a matter-of-fact tone, not as a big deal.
3. Never punish the child for bedwetting. It is punishment enough as it is. No child is pleased with himself for doing this. Children who act as if they don't care are probably those who feel the worst about it, or who have the hardest time facing it. Punishment won't help them to do this. Encouragement will.
4. Never shame or humiliate a child who has wet the bed. Of course it is more work for you, but humiliation won't help him get past this any faster.
5. No matter how thrilled you are about a dry night, try to leave this success as the child's. Your excitement and praise can all too easily backfire into more pressure. Your child is bound to figure out that if you are so pleased with a dry night, you will be equally displeased with a wet one. A quiet nod of approval from a parent is plenty. Leave the job up to your child and let him learn to take pride in his own achievement.

feel helpless and inadequate. If there are signs in the child of depression or of hopelessness, he should be evaluated and helped by a professional. Treatment early can prevent a serious sense of failure in this area.

Body Exploration

When his diaper comes off a baby may arch forward to look down. A boy will see his penis and be curious. Reaching down with both hands, he starts to pull on it. An erection! By now, his whole body is involved. He arches forward, pulls on his penis affectionately. His mother is a bit shocked. Just as he starts to urinate, she drops the diaper at his penis. He flops back onto the changing table, chortling gleefully. His mother's face is red. She calls her husband at work to interrupt him and recount the episode. "What should I have done?"

When a baby girl's diaper is removed, she is likely to "find herself." At a time of being undiapered, she may pass warm urine. Her face glows. She squirms and reaches down to find the warm spot. A finger enters her vagina. She explores herself. Her father has been changing her. Alarmed, he reaches for her hand to pull it away. He calls his wife. "Is it okay for a 2-year-old to put her fingers in her vagina? Will she hurt herself?" (He is thinking that her hymen might be damaged.) His wife assures him that little girls have always "played" with themselves, and that there isn't any reason to be alarmed.

As children discover their bodies, changing diapers can become more complicated. Should you try to stop the investigation? I don't think so. Does masturbation hurt a child? Not that I know of. The more you try to interfere, the more you are likely to heighten the excitement. Later, you can help your child understand that masturbation should be confined to a private place at home. For now, your best hope of preparing him to keep his self-exploration private later on is for you to honor his privacy. If you can keep your reaction to yourself, both boys and girls are more likely to learn to keep their masturbation to themselves.

Childcare and Toilet Training

Parents, teachers, and other childcare providers (at home or in a childcare center) will need to come to a common understanding: A child's motivation for toilet training comes from his wish to be like the important adults in his life. His parents or older siblings are most likely to be the models for this big effort. If he is close to caregivers or nursery school teachers, he may look up to them and want to imitate or please them as well.

But these caregivers are less likely to be included in the routines of daily life—the child probably won't have a chance to observe a teacher on the potty! Those who care for the child need to understand that parents must guide the steps that are introduced as he works on toilet training. It is up to the parents to watch for the child's signs of readiness to know when each toilet training step should be offered to him.

With this understanding, toilet training has a far better chance of being addressed consistently by all of the adults. Any inconsistency is bound to leave a child feeling confused. If parents and child have already turned toilet training into a battle, disagreements among the adults will only make it worse.

Preschool teachers and other care providers will have their own reasons for wanting the child to achieve success in toilet training. (The child will sense these and try to meet their goals. If the child is not yet ready, he runs the risk of giving up.) Unfortunately "gatekeeping" (the natural competitive feelings of adults who care for a child) will surface for adults who care for the same child when it is time for toilet training. Caregivers might think, "If they'd only try to train him my way, we'd be successful." This kind of competition with parents may color the caregiver's attitude toward the child's efforts. For example, "He's not even trying because he knows his parents will let him get away with it." The child will "know" that he's not living up to the caregiver's or teacher's wishes. If they matter to him, he'll feel discouraged that he can't please them.

Since "gatekeeping" is so predictable—especially for major developmental steps like toilet training, parents and caregivers can expect it and be prepared for it. It is essential that they discuss the steps toward the child's success in toilet training before any disagreement comes to the child's attention. In addition, they will need to recognize what their combination of expectations mean to the child in the way of pressure to perform. He must please all of them—and the cost to him will be that using the potty is no longer *his* goal, but giving in to theirs. Is that what you want?

My best advice is to be open about your own passion for doing what you believe is right for your child, and also let other caregivers know that you value the passion they bring to caring for your child. Showing this kind of respect can help reduce the tension and bitter feelings that such competition can stir up. Then, even when you disagree, you will be able to use your shared concern for your child's well-being to find common ground.

Toilet Training in a Childcare Center or Nursery School

Teachers and caregivers have their own pressures—so many different children at different stages of development. Here are some ways for them to cope with the demands of caring for many children at once, while also respecting each child's stage of development:

1. Have a bathroom setup that is child-oriented, with a small toilet and other interesting things to do there—books to read, a picture to look at, a pad for drawing while each child sits.
2. An adult who is *not* under pressure to see a child trained and can serve just as a companion should be available to accompany the child to the bathroom.
3. No adult talk in the classroom about toilet training. Other children can ask "Are you dry?" "Do you still use diapers?" Don't enter into it with them. This is an effort on their part to understand themselves—by comparing themselves with other children.
4. Be ready to accept each child where he is in these steps toward mastery. Be ready to admire each little step he tries out.

(continued on next page)

Toilet Training in a Childcare Center or Nursery School
(continued from previous page)

But let each success be his, and don't advertise them to any-one else. Ask him if he'd like to tell his parents when they come to pick him up. If he doesn't, respect his wishes. He'll let them know soon enough on his own.

5. Privately discuss with parents where their child is in his progress and what he is doing. Keep separate notes for each family, so you can be sure not to confuse them.

6. Have a routine time (after circle time) when any child who wants to go to the potty can line up, try it, and be quietly commended. But the other children need to be respected for "not going." "I know you'll go when you're ready." Offer them a parallel activity that is not too interesting, but respects the fact that all children are not ready.

7. Plan a parent evening when both parents and caregivers can let off steam about setbacks, share ideas, and express their own wishes. Parents can give each other much needed support. Aim this evening at an understanding of the steps of toilet training, and each child's needs to be in charge of his own goals.

8. Recognize, as a teacher or childcare provider, that you are hungry for the child's success, and that this hunger can lead to pressure on the child—and on the parent. Early toilet training is highly overrated as a sign of success in our society. But children started early (between 17 and 27 months) often don't master toilet training until they are the same age as children who start a little later. Why risk the feelings of failure when there is plenty of time? We need to be aware that children can succeed when they are ready—with our direction, but not our pressure.

Constipation, Soiling, Megacolon

How to Tell If Your Child Has Constipation: A constipated child will have hard bowel movements that cause pain on the way out. Often a constipated child will also have a stomachache, and lose his appetite. Sometimes there can even be fresh red blood on the surface of a bowel movement that was hard enough to tear the membranes in the child's anus. A constipated child will move his bowels less often than usual, but what is usual for one child may not be for another. Some children (and adults) pass stools several times a day, and others only once every few days.

Soiling: Too many children respond to the pressure to be toilet trained with constipation. Although they may have initially accepted routines, and appear to be using the toilet, they may unconsciously begin to hold back. The result is a hardened stool. The longer the child goes without moving his bowels, the larger and harder the stool becomes. Eventually, liquid bowel movement leaks around the hardened stool, staining diapers or underwear.

A parent is bound to think this is diarrhea, when it is in fact just the opposite. If a parent tries to stop what she mistakenly thinks of as diarrhea (for example, with rice water or other home remedies, elimination of fruit juice and fiber, or medicines to control diarrhea), the constipation will of course only become more severe.

Chronic Constipation (Encopresis): As bowel movements become larger and larger, and are retained longer and longer, the child's intestine is stretched and becomes less able to push the bowel movements toward the rectum. Very quickly the process—pain, withholding, leaking around the constipated stool, stretched and weakened intestines, and fear of having a bowel movement—becomes a vicious cycle. This vicious cycle is referred to as chronic constipation (*encopresis*).

With constipation and then liquid leaking, you can be sure the child has a hard stool that may hurt his anal sphincter when he tries to pass it. The child's fear of pain is likely to cause further tightening of his anal sphincter. The first step, with your pediatrician's involvement, is to use stool softeners given by mouth to help your child empty his rectum of stool. Your child will need you to reassure him that with this medicine he can move his bowels without pain. "This medicine will make your poop soft so they won't hurt you." You must offer help for both the physical (hard, painful stools) and psychological (fear of pain) aspects of such severe constipation.

When to Worry: Constipation is common, and sometimes runs in families. At least 10 percent of all children go through periods of constipation. But when the child's stools begin to be less frequent, and when they harden, a parent needs to pay attention. A hard bowel movement can hurt. It can cause a small, superficial, but painful tear called an anal fissure. Then a child will begin to withhold bowel movements in order to avoid the pain.

Though constipation is common, occasionally it can be a sign of a more serious medical condition (for example, appendicitis, hypothyroidism, lead poisoning, celiac disease, and

Hirschsprung's megacolon disease). In these cases other symptoms are usually present as well. Some medications can also cause constipation. If a child who seems constipated develops severe abdominal pain, a fever, bloody stools, or vomiting, call your pediatrician right away to be sure that there isn't a more serious medical problem. If the usual remedies for constipation (some of which are described below) haven't worked, then it is important to ask your child's doctor to check for medical conditions that can cause constipation.

If a child withholds his stools and develops constipation, his large bowel (colon) begins to expand with the retained feces. Over time, the colon can lose the muscle tone that is necessary to be effective in pushing bowel movements along and out. This condition, stools retained for a week or so in a toddler, can lead to a temporarily enlarged and weakened colon (called megacolon). As with chronic constipation, brownish fluid begins to leak around the hard, stuck bowel movement. As we said, this is not diarrhea. You can feel the full intestine when you press into the child's left lower abdomen. The child may complain of pain as you press, or as he tries to have a stool.

When you seek medical advice, many clinics recommend enemas or suppositories that are likely to add to the child's resistance about having a bowel movement. In most cases, though, it was his resistance that caused the megacolon in the first place. I believe that when this is the case, any treatment offered must take into account the child's resistance and respect his protectiveness about this part of his body. Try the measures outlined below for constipation before you use any intrusive methods. If the doctor feels that they are necessary, prepare the child and reassure him that he will feel better and not need these measures later. If he becomes very anxious or resistant, psychological counseling can help.

What To Do: Constipation that has only just begun can often be helped with attention to a child's diet, and increased fluids and activity, if no other symptoms are present. Lack of fluids or of fibrous fruits, vegetables, and grains is often a part of the problem. A parent can try to introduce more fluids, especially fruit juices, and more activity, and cut back on junk food (their refined sugar and flour fills a child up without leaving room for the fiber he needs to keep his bowels moving). But the child may resist, especially if such foods are new to him.

Dietary adjustments are important. But if a food battle is looming, it can and should be avoided when you and your child are already contending with the child's constipation. Instead, call your physician to see if she'll recommend a bowel softener and/or a mild laxative. Daily doses are usually needed until the bowel movements are softened. Then, diet changes can be introduced more gradually, when the stress of constipation has begun to subside.

Some physicians suggest enemas or suppositories. But unless it is absolutely necessary and unavoidable, it is far better to leave this private and vulnerable part of the child's body alone. Enemas and, to a lesser extent, suppositories can seem threatening to a small child and can add to his resistance to defecating.

The pain or discomfort at the anal sphincter can be decreased by applying a small amount of petroleum jelly or vitamin A and D ointment. The child can even be given a dab on a cotton ball so that he can put it on this area himself. This will help him understand where and why he is hurting and that it can be helped. It also leaves him in control of this private and now more vulnerable area.

How to recognize constipation:

- Hardened, dried-out bowel movements, sometimes with fresh blood around them
- Passing stools causes pain in the anal and rectal region but makes a stomachache go away
- Child loses interest in eating

How to treat constipation:

- Let up on pressure to be trained
- Increase fluids
- Add fibrous food or fruit and vegetables
- More physical activity—make it daily

Call the child's physician or nurse practitioner if the above measures do not work soon. He or she may check for other causes of constipation and may also recommend:

- stool softener
- mild laxative
- petroleum jelly at anal opening

Children need the reassurance that parents do know how to help. They may need parents to assure them that with the stool softener and petroleum jelly, the bowel movement will be soft and won't hurt. And, most important of all, they need an apology from parents about the pressure on them to be trained. A parent might say: "I'm sorry I pushed you to go to the toilet. You can have a diaper (or training pants) when you want to go. You can use the diaper to have a softer bowel movement so it won't hurt so much. We don't have to flush your poop away." This last statement may seem surprising, and unnecessary. But it is an offer that may relieve him.

If there are new pressures on the child, such as a new baby, or a move, or a parent who is away from home, let him know you understand that they are bothering him. This, in turn, will help him understand his own "touchpoint"—or backward step and new adjustment. All of these steps may be necessary daily until his stools are soft and he has regained a regular routine for moving his bowels.

How a Child Understands Constipation: A child's understanding of his body and how it works changes as he grows. Very young children give little thought to what they cannot see or feel. For most children under age 4, constipation mostly means a painful belly and sometimes a sore butt.

By 4, some children may be struggling to understand where the food they put in their mouths goes, and where the poop that comes out "at the other end" comes from. Though they may have been told that there is a connection, it will of course

Foods that won't help or can increase constipation:

- breads made with refined flour
- potatoes
- white rice
- pasta made with refined flour
- cheese
- bananas, and sometimes even apples
- cow's milk, especially when first introduced

Foods that may help relieve constipation:

- prune juice
- most fruits and vegetables; though raisins and prunes are favorites, apricots and peaches are also very helpful
- fruit juices, especially prune juice, though many children won't like the taste
- whole-grain breads, pastas, and cereals, for example, raisin bran

Other remedies:

- encourage the child with constipation to drink lots of fluids, especially water and fruit juice
- encourage regular physical activity: running, climbing a jungle gym, peddling a tricycle or bike

be very difficult for them to imagine how food "turns" into poop. They may already, though, begin to worry that if food keeps coming in and poop doesn't come out, a person could literally blow up like a balloon and explode.

By 6 or 7, children may begin to develop more elaborate explanations for the mechanics behind this remarkable transformation—of food into poop.

How to Talk About Constipation with a Child: Very young children have not learned to be embarrassed about their bodily functions—this is something that they will later learn from adults. Instead, they are curious, and proud.

As early as 4 years, though, many children are quite aware of the expectations of the adults and peers around them not to soil their underwear. Already, parents will encounter a child's embarrassment and shame if they mention this topic. Of course parents will want to avoid adding to the child's shame by further humiliating or punishing him.

Instead, listen to the child: What is it about the problem that bothers him? What is the face-saving explanation he has invented for himself? Let him hold onto this—he probably knows perfectly well what really happened, and will appreciate your respect for his predicament. Offer him help for the part of the problem that concerns him. Let him participate in thinking up his own face-saving solution. One colleague we admire who specializes in helping children with encopresis told us about a little boy who explained that all he needed was a different-colored toilet and then he could start using it again. He was really saying that he needed to save face, and an excuse to get out from under the pressure that had led to his troubles.

When a part of a young child's body hurts him, for example—when he is constipated—his belly or his anus, he may feel that his body is "broken" or worry how he'll ever be put back together again. Without an understanding of how his body works, the young child is more likely to have trouble putting his worries into perspective and can become quite frantic, or preoccupied. He may even make up his own way of looking at what is happening to his body, and he is likely to blame himself. Explain in simple terms what is happening and why fruit, liquids, and exercise can help.

Young children also seem to be easily overwhelmed by pain—having fewer coping mechanisms for handling it, and more frightened by pain because they cannot readily understand what started it, how long it will last, and whether and when it will stop. It is no wonder, then, that a young child with constipation will quickly struggle to regain control of the pain he feels by refusing to move his bowels. It also is easy to see why simple information about the predictable ways the human body works, and heals, can be helpful even for very young children. There are a number of clear and entertaining books about bodily functions (see Bibliography) that can help straighten out the confusion.

Diapers: Cloth or Disposable

Cloth Diapers: Many parents wonder about what kind of diapers to use. Cloth diapers are so soft, and smell so wholesome. They seem like an easy solution if they are supplied by a company that picks up dirty diapers and delivers fresh ones. But the dirty diapers do pile up, and can smell until they are collected. Water with a bit of vinegar in the receptacle helps keep down odors.

If you have the energy, you can wash your own—in a soft detergent. Some babies are sensitive to certain detergents. If you use cloth diapers and your baby develops a rash in the diaper area, remember detergent sensitivity as a possibility. With cloth diapers, plastic pants are necessary to contain the "overflow." But frequent changes will be necessary, because plastic pants can hold in the ammonia from urine, and irritate the baby's skin.

Disposable Diapers: Many parents in the United States have chosen disposable diapers, though they are expensive and clog up our landfills. (In some highly populated countries, such a shift would be an ecological catastrophe.) But parents who prefer them feel that disposable diapers are easier to change, and appreciate that they can take dirty ones out with the trash. When they fit well, the baby is not likely to leak around them to wet or soil parents as they cuddle him.

But the plastic around the paper diaper can be too effective, trapping the ammonia from urine the way plastic pants do. A diaper rash may certainly result. Many disposable diapers, though, are pretreated with an anti-ammonia agent that may help to combat diaper rashes.

Disposable diapers make up 4 or 5 percent of the garbage that goes into our nation's landfills—annually contributing an estimated 5 million tons of untreated human waste and 2 billion tons overall when you include the plastic and paper of disposables. They also leach environmental contaminants as well as human waste, which can threaten groundwater and nearby streams and rivers. So many babies using so many diapers is surely a threat to our environment. In their defense, the disposable diaper manufacturers argue that cloth diapers take their toll too, with the hot water and soap it takes to wash them. But then disposables require lots of water and plastic and paper in their manufacture, for a product that is used once.

The choice between cloth and disposable diapers will be a family's choice. (Childcare providers are likely to voice their preference too.) Though an individual baby may do better with one kind than another (for example, due to a detergent sensitivity, one infant may be less prone to rashes in disposable diapers), cloth vs. disposable generally makes little difference to babies. The choice may matter more to these babies when they are grown and must contend with the environment that we have left them!

Diaper Rash

Diaper rash occurs in all babies. It's a pimply rash that may appear suddenly and is scattered. It cannot be completely avoided and may appear even after meticulous cleanliness. But here are a few suggestions for cutting down on how often diaper rash occurs, how severe it becomes, and for avoiding a few other rashes that can affect infants in diapers.

How to Cut Back on Diaper Rash

1. I have recommended that parents use petroleum jelly after each cleanup of stool and urine. This usually helps prevent a rash because the grease keeps moisture that can cause diaper rash away from the baby's skin. "Unpetroleum jelly," is available in natural food stores for those concerned about petroleum derivatives.

2. Frequent changes can cut down on diaper rash by limiting the time the baby's skin is exposed to moisture, and irritants in urine and stool. It helps a great deal to change diapers soon after each bowel movement, and every few hours.

3. Be sure not to wash and wipe your child's skin too often—this can cause dryness and make the skin vulnerable to breakdown. When you do wash and wipe after a bowel movement, be careful to pat the skin dry and avoid vigorous rubbing.

4. Though powder in the diaper may sop up the ammonia from urine, many powders can build up along a baby's skin creases and then cause skin breakdown. Breathing in powder, especially talcum, can cause respiratory problems. Talcum powder is not safe for babies, so corn starch has replaced it. But I do not recommend these products.

5. When a rash is already present, zinc oxide cream or ointment makes a protective coating so the rash can heal.

6. Be sure to give your baby's skin a chance to air and avoid retaining moisture. Stay away from clothing such as plastic underwear, which can hold moisture in.

7. It's wonderful in warm weather to be able to air babies' bottoms. They love it. They'll kick and squirm with pleasure. Older babies begin to explore themselves at such an uncovered time. Don't be surprised or horrified.

Sometimes diaper rash can be caused or worsened by irritants in the diapers themselves (or from the soap that cloth diapers are laundered in), in baby wipes, or in lotions and creams meant to protect the skin. If your baby's diaper rash won't go away or is getting worse, try the following steps.

When a Diaper Rash Won't Go Away

1. Try a different kind of diaper, or if you use cloth diapers, try washing them in a mild, hypo-allergenic soap or detergent.
2. Stop using baby wipes and try using a gentle cloth with lukewarm water and a mild, hypo-allergenic soap.
3. Stop using the lotion or cream you'd been applying to your baby's skin after changes or baths. Instead, try using a simple moisture repellent ointment such as petroleum jelly or vitamin A and D ointment, and be sure that these are unscented.
4. Talk it over with your baby's pediatrician. She or he certainly has had plenty of experience helping parents fight diaper rash. The pediatrician will also want to be sure that a rash that isn't responding to usual remedies isn't caused by something else (for example, thrush, impetigo—see below).

Here are a few other kinds of common rashes that can appear in the diaper area:

Thrush (Candida albicans)
What It Looks Like: Thrush causes a severe red rash. It looks raw, and seems almost hopeless to heal with ordinary remedies

such as the ones usually prescribed. This is not a normal diaper rash, which is a scattered sprinkling of tiny red spots. This more upsetting rash has larger, new, red blotches with distinct, raised borders. This sore-looking rash does not appear to bother the baby as much as it does the parent. A very common infection, caused by a fungus, this rash is more likely after a baby has taken antibiotics. The antibiotics kill the bacteria that normally live in the mouth and digestive system, making room for the fungus to move in.

Often this kind of infection begins in a baby's mouth (especially in the first 6 months), where it looks like a white, filmy covering and can cause enough soreness to interfere with feedings. Then the infection sometimes travels all the way through the digestive system to cause a rash around the baby's buttocks. A breastfeeding mother's nipples may also get infected—ouch!

What To Do: Thrush won't just go away. Ask your doctor for a fungicidal ointment. With such an ointment, this kind of rash should disappear and heal over several days. Even if it returns, you'll be confident about how to treat it. If it doesn't improve, be sure to tell your child's pediatrician, as sometimes another kind of ointment is needed. Drops for the infant's mouth and ointment for the baby's bottom and for nursing mother's breast may be necessary to attack the infection—all at once.

Be sure to sterilize bottle nipples and pacifiers as these may harbor the fungus that causes this infection. If your child is on antibiotics, find out from your pediatrician if he is ready for yogurts that contain naturally occurring bacteria. These may help get normal bacteria growing in the child's digestive system, making it harder for the fungus to thrive there.

Impetigo

What It Looks Like: This is a rash that commonly occurs in older children and on parts of the body beyond the diaper area. But since it can occur whenever there is skin breakdown, it certainly can occur in infants in the diaper area. It looks quite different from the large numbers of tiny little red spots sprinkled across the buttocks, thighs, and genitals that appear with diaper rash.

Impetigo—an infection of the skin by common strep or staph bacteria (staphylococcus, streptococcus)—first appears as a few larger sores that may appear anywhere on the infant's body, but often on the back, stomach, and buttocks. They are a darker red, almost brown color, and ooze a small amount of yellow fluid that forms a crust. Because this fluid contains the infecting bacteria, these sores can easily spread if they are touched—to other parts of the body, and to other people.

What To Do: Call your doctor about the rash. He or she is likely to prescribe an anti-bacterial ointment, or even, for more severe or long-lasting cases, an antibiotic to take by mouth. You'll want to cover the sores with the ointment as often as the doctor says (usually at least two or three times a day and after bathing). After touching them be sure to wash your hands with soapy warm water. If you can't keep your baby from scratching the sores, cut his fingernails short, wash his hands frequently, and keep other people from touching the sores. Keep the baby's towels and clothing separate from everyone else's.

Because these blisterlike sores are caused by bacteria, your baby may also have a fever. Rarely, impetigo can be a sign of a more serious infection—if your baby has a fever, vomiting, or darkened urine with these sores, call your doctor right away. Even if none of these other symptoms is present, you'll still want to seek your doctor's advice, especially for small babies.

Diarrhea

How to Tell If Your Child Has Diarrhea: One loose stool alone is not worth worrying about. But frequent loose, watery stools (more than four a day) are a cause for concern. Continuous loose bowel movements, painful BMs, or BMs that contain blood or mucus certainly should be reported to your physician.

Some Common Causes of Diarrhea: Diarrhea may be caused by an infection. Viral infections are the commonest cause for diarrhea. Usually this kind of diarrhea will last for a few days, and goes away by itself without any special treatment. Be sure, though, to give lots of fluids and watch for signs of dehydration (see page 82).

Another common cause of diarrhea is treatment with antibiotics, for example, for an ear infection. Sometimes this can be prevented or reduced by feeding a child yogurt that contains naturally occurring bacteria. The digestive system normally harbors bacteria that cause no harm. When antibiotics wipe these out, less benign bacteria can take over. Introducing the healthy bacteria in yogurt (check the label to be sure that the yogurt you buy does contain "active cultures") back into a child's digestive system appears to help restore the balance.

A more severe form of diarrhea can be due to a bacterial infection. Bacteria that are not normally present in the digestive system may be taken in with contaminated food—leading to food poisoning. Treatment with antibiotics is necessary for some bacterial and also parasitic infections.

The child's diet or an allergy to foods are other possible causes and may require dietary adjustments. If loose stools continue for a long period, they could be a symptom of some kind of food intolerance. They could be indicating a milk allergy, usually lactose—a sugar contained in milk—intolerance, and less commonly a reaction to milk protein. A soybean milk may be necessary, along with avoidance of cow's milk products (for example, cheeses, yogurt, ice cream). Gluten, contained in wheat, barley, and rye, is poorly tolerated by children with celiac disease, another cause for diarrhea. There are a number of more unusual causes for diarrhea, including infection by parasites, or illnesses such as cystic fibrosis and inflammatory bowel disease (see Appendix, *Resources for Parents*). The watery fluid that can leak when a child is very constipated is *not* diarrhea. (See "Constipation.")

Dehydration: In a child with frequent loose bowel movements, the doctor will also want to check for dehydration. Dehydration means that the child has lost—usually from diarrhea or vomiting—the fluid that his body requires. The doctor will look for dry mouth and lips, dull eyes, infrequent wet diapers or urination, darker urine, even dry skin and—in an infant—a sunken soft spot. Diarrhea causes loss of fluid, making a child feel weak and dizzy. This needs to be taken care of promptly.

Usually a child can make up for fluid loss by drinking lots of soothing liquids (see page 85), but when the fluid loss is severe and the child is too ill to drink, hospitalization and intravenous liquids (given by a needle placed in a vein) may be necessary. If a young child is vomiting as well as having diarrhea, he will be even more likely to need prompt medical attention and treatment. Hot weather, or a fever, can also increase a child's risk of dehydration. The younger the child, the more vulnerable to dehydration he will be. The younger the child, the faster you will need to act to help him to take in gentle fluids that his body can hold onto, and to reach out to his doctor for help.

How to tell if your child is dehydrated:

- dry lips, tongue, and mouth
- dull, glazed eyes
- faster heartbeat
- less frequent urination or, in an infant, fewer wet diapers
- darker urine color
- dry skin
- in an infant, sunken soft spot (fontanelle)
- less playful, irritable
- tired, weak, dizzy

If you see these signs of dehydration in your child, call your doctor right away.

What to Do If Your Child Has Diarrhea:

- Increase clear liquids to prevent or treat dehydration—sips of sweetened fluids every 10–15 minutes. Your doctor may suggest one of several over-the-counter drinks that you can give your child to combat dehydration caused by diarrhea. Ginger ale left open a little while—until it goes flat—is also often a big help.
- Watch for signs of dehydration—listlessness, temperature, dull eyes, and dry mucous membranes.
- Check diapers to determine how often your child is urinating. If there is no urine for more than a few hours you will want to offer him liquids to drink more often. If there is no urine for 6 hours or more, call your child's pediatrician.
- Change your child's diapers frequently to prevent diarrhea from causing skin breakdown.
- Use petroleum jelly or even zinc oxide ointment after gently washing stool from your child's bottom with warm, soapy water and a soft cloth. Gently pat him dry before putting on the ointment—his skin is likely to be a little raw, so try not to rub it too energetically.
- Be sure to wash your hands (and your child's hands) frequently, and after each diaper change or contact with his stool. Wash your hands again before touching other children, food, or food utensils. Diarrhea caused by an infection is highly contagious and easily spread.

- Call your child's doctor to report any signs of dehydration, stomachaches, and mucus or blood mixed with the diarrhea.
- Don't give your child over-the-counter diarrhea remedies unless your pediatrician instructs you to do so.
- If you must take time off from work to be at home with your child, try to turn this into a special time to be together. Your child will always cherish these times when you nurtured him through sickness.

If Your Child Is Also Vomiting:

- **Call your doctor.**
- Pay even more attention to the signs of dehydration.
- Work harder to get your child to take fluids, but let his digestive system settle a little before each try.
- Try waiting 15–30 minutes after your child vomits before giving him a sip or two of liquid, ideally one of the over-the-counter drinks designed to replace the salts lost with diarrhea and vomiting.
- Wait another 5 or 10 minutes before giving him another two or three sips.
- Then give one teaspoon every 5 minutes for the first hour.
- For the second hour, increase the amount to one tablespoon every 5–10 minutes.
- By the third hour, try to give your child one ounce every 10–15 minutes.

- Gradually help him work his way up to about 4 to 6 ounces of fluid each hour until he's recovered.
- If he vomits again, start over, but also be sure to call his doctor—again.

Fluids to prevent or counteract dehydration:

- water: 8 ounces of water mixed with 1/2 teaspoon of salt and sugar to taste
- over-the-counter liquids designed for infants and children, such as Pedialyte and Ricelyte: consult your pediatrician
- flat ginger ale
- chicken or other broths with salt
- any mild, noncreamy soup

The salt in soups and broths is important: It helps the child's body retain fluid. For mild cases of diarrhea, there is no need to stop breastfeeding or milk formulas. Breast milk and formula can provide necessary fluid.

Foods that can make diarrhea worse:

- any drink or food containing caffeine (for example, many soda drinks)
- many fruits and vegetables
- if there is a milk allergy, milk products can cause or aggravate diarrhea

(continued on next page)

(continued from previous page)

Foods that may slow down diarrhea:

- toast (white bread)
- rice
- crackers
- mashed potatoes
- bananas
- yogurt with naturally occurring bacteria

Traditional remedies:

- In some cultures, rice water is prepared for small babies with diarrhea by saving the leftover water after boiling rice. Don't let all the water boil off. Be sure the rice water is not too hot before serving. It can be sweetened with a little honey, and add ½ teaspoon of salt for 8 ounces.
- Some herb teas can be soothing for an irritated belly, especially chamomile and mint teas, but many teas actually cause increased urination and loss of fluids—the opposite of what is needed with diarrhea and dehydration
(See also flat ginger ale and chicken broth above.)

Fear of Flushing

Fear of flushing the toilet is common in 2- and 3-year-old children as they work on toilet training. A child this age worries about losing a part of himself—and he thinks of his bowel movements as part of his body.

At this age he has also just been through a major test of his independence—in separating from his parents with his recent ability to walk away from them. For this, he has had to rely on an earlier achievement—object permanence: the new ability to "see" something in his "mind's eye" when it is not visible, and understand that something (including his parents) can still exist even when he can't see it. He has tested and tried out this new ability to help him make these separations possible.

But he's still in the process of mastering separation. "If I leave my father, will he leave me?" Then, as he goes along with the major achievement of toilet training, the child can't help but wonder: "Where is my poop going? Why should I give it up? What if I fall in and go there too?" (Children with overly acute hearing—auditory hypersensitivity—may even be terrified of the sound of the flushing.) These fears may seem absurd to parents, who may want to push the child to overcome them. Wait. If he seems afraid, do not flush his stools away while he is present. Give him time.

At this same age, a child often worries about the swirling water of the bathtub drain. "Where's the water going, daddy? Will I go down the drain too?" Even the sound of the drain as it snorts down the water frightens some children.

As a child gets more comfortable with his toilet training, after several months of complying and of feeling competent in this area, he may be ready to watch a parent flush the toilet. He may want to flush it himself. Over and over. But, don't push it yet. He may try to play out his fear with clay or modeling dough. Be careful, as he may also want to put nondisposable materials down the toilet and plug up your drain. Eventually, he will show you that he's ready to watch his own bowel movement go down. He may still be fearful but fascinated. I'd certainly urge parents to take his fear seriously until he's ready to master it.

Preschool Pressure

Most preschools won't accept children until they are out of diapers. (See "Childcare and Toilet Training" for dealing with daycare centers and at-home childcare providers.) Of course it is easier and more sanitary not to have to change the diapers of 3- or 4-year-olds in a group. But the pressure on children—often as young as 2 years, 9 months—who must be trained early to qualify for childcare interferes with their need to give up diapers at their own pace. Such pressure is all too likely to backfire. When children can't make toilet training their own job, they are likely to resist, for example, by withholding urine and bowel movements.

According to the *Children's Hospital Guide to Your Child's Health and Development*, 40 percent of 3-year-olds still use diapers. Must childcare centers and preschools ignore the developmental needs of so many children? When faced with their requirements, parents are bound to take them to mean that their child should be trained by now: "He's 3 years old. The other kids there must be trained already." Parents will then begin to rush their child. He may accept the pressure to be clean and dry for his parents' sake, or he may resist.

If he is unable to comply with the pressure, the child is bound to feel ashamed of his "failure." This may be the start of problems. What parent would want to take the chance? I would like to see parents and professionals join together to change preschool policies and eliminate this unnecessary pressure on children and leave the timing of toilet training to the child.

When a child has been recently trained, parents and teachers need to agree on expectations and dealing with accidents. When a child is still struggling to master toilet training, conflicting messages from these different important adults can add to his struggle. Parents and providers will need to agree on routines and expectations for the child. In order for this to occur, parents and teacher must become a "team"—with the child's best interests as their shared goal. (See discussion of "gatekeeping" in "Childcare and Toilet Training.")

Meanwhile, do not be surprised if your child still needs diapers at home, though he can go without them at school. The teacher may say, "He has no problem using the toilet at school. I wonder why he does at home." You may feel that the teacher is taking credit for your child's success, and criticizing you. But you know how much it is costing him to comply at school, and how he needs to relax at home—where he's safe. Your child may need your reassurance: "You can use diapers at home. I know that you're proud to stay dry at school. But you can wear them at home if you need to." Try to mean it. Otherwise, you convey more pressure than he can master. You may well feel the competition from school. But don't let this work against doing what is best for your child.

By 4 years of age, children in preschool feel even more pressure from each other to be toilet trained: "Are you dry? Do you *ever* use diapers?" Combined with the teacher's and parental pressure, this can work in one of two ways. He may try very hard to be "grown up," and to please peers and teachers by using the toilet. Or he may give up. In the latter case, his self-image can be at risk.

Helping Your Child Handle Preschool Pressure

1. If you can, find a preschool that accepts 3-year-olds in diapers.
2. If you can find such a school, discuss with your child's teacher your decision to let your child set the pace of toilet training. Listen to her or his objections and concerns first, and then share your own. Be sure you both are in agreement.
3. If your child is just trained and attends a school where this is required, you still need to discuss how the teacher will deal with an occasional "accident."
4. If your child is not yet trained, consider finding a childcare center or at-home care (family care) that permits diapers until the child becomes trained at his own pace.
5. If your child is still in diapers or has an accident and reports to you that he was teased at school "for still being a baby," do not respond with more pressure. You might say, "Lots of kids talk like this. They have been through this too. You know that you have to be the boss of your own toilet training. You'll get there when you're ready." He may look at you in wonder—at the respect you have conveyed. Your respect and gentle encouragement may help him make his own efforts—and they will be *his*.

Pressure from Grandparents and Others

New parents can be surprisingly vulnerable to advice from others, especially grandparents. Many have a story about the pressure they felt from their parents or in-laws, or competitive friends to "get going" with toilet training. "Grandparent pressure" is not, of course, saved up for toilet training alone. But parents are especially vulnerable to their advice on any highly prized step in a child's development, and toilet training is certainly a major one.

You may want to take the advice of others sometimes. It's not always bad. Sometimes it can even be reassuring to know you can fall back on your family's traditions or other sources of wisdom. But if you want to make your own decision, you'll need to take a step back. To stand their ground, parents need to agree on a plan for their child's toilet training. After you have agreed and taken your child's abilities and temperament into account, you are ready to start. When you do, try to resist signals from others around you to whom you are vulnerable, so that you can be open to your child's signals. If you feel confused, this confusion is all too easily transmitted to the child. Any child is likely to be clearer about the task of toilet training if his parents are not confused. This is one reason for parents to decide on these steps at home and by themselves.

Grandparents who are raising or helping to raise their own grandchildren must often come to an even more difficult decision. "Will I raise this child like I was raised—or should I follow the methods his parents prefer?" I would suggest that grandparents, too, sort out their confusion to avoid transmitting it to the child. Then, steps toward toilet training can be presented quietly and respectfully—remembering that each child is different. Your grandchild may need to use you as a target for his own feelings, and these may make him even more likely to resist a step like toilet training: "You're not my parent! I don't have to do what you tell me!" A grandparent raising a grandchild can answer, "I am raising you now, but I am not going to tell you when or how you'll learn to use the toilet. That'll be your job, not mine. But I do want you to respect me, and to listen to the ways that I can help you learn something as difficult as toilet training." When parents and grandparents are sharing the care of a child, it is even more important to address an approach together. (See also "Preschool Pressure.")

Sibling Rivalry and Setbacks

Among the predictable times when an already trained older child is likely to have a setback is the arrival of a new sibling or even before. During his mother's pregnancy a child watches his mother's belly swell and is bound to feel confused. At this age, he wants to be just like her. His confusion and his need to identify with his mother can often lead to attempts to withhold his stools—as if he could fill himself up—"like mommy"—by not letting anything go. Constipation can be one way to "be like mommy," among others. He's bound to try to walk "like mommy," to get up from his chair with a groan, to eat more to "get fat like mommy." A wise parent will understand and accept these behaviors, and help him accept his wish "to be like mommy." If he's constipated, he may need a bowel softener in addition to the reassurance a parent can offer that wishes such as these are natural. They will pass.

When the new baby is brought home, many 2- or 3-year-old siblings begin to wet their pants or to hide to have a stool. Just as they may want to nurse, or to drink out of a bottle "like baby," they are likely to want to wet and soil and wear diapers again too. If your child does this, offer him diapers or training pants again. Be sure you change him with the same loving, fun interaction with which you approach the new baby's changing table. He is likely to be highly sensitive to any difference in your attitude. Of course, his stools will be smellier. Of course, you are disappointed with his wet underwear. But, remember his reason—conscious or unconscious. He is trying to be the doted-upon baby he had once been, though you have given that baby up for another. Reassure him that you value him for the older child he has become, but that you can accept his need to be your baby again sometimes too. Otherwise, he too may see his wetting and soiling as a failure. Then this behavior may take on a life of its own.

Emphasize special times with you "without the baby." The next most likely setback will be at the time when the baby starts to crawl, or to toddle, to get into the older child's toys. Everyone adores the baby—"He's so darling when he crawls or walks." No one thinks the gangly, awkward, angry older one is darling any more. Of course, he is likely to regress—again.

Handling Setbacks When a New Sibling Arrives

1. Understand the child's regression as normal.
2. Help him understand it: "Of course you'd like to be like the baby and get everyone's attention. We all would."
3. Reassure him: "You'll stop wetting or soiling. Don't worry. You can go back into diapers or training pants so you don't need to worry. When you're ready, we can try again. But, meanwhile we'll have our changing times together."
4. Emphasize special times with you—reading to him at night, going to the store with him, playing a game together. Save a special time with him alone. Do this at least once a week. Talk about it the rest of the week. It's an opportunity to make up to him for his feeling that you are deserting him.

Standing to Urinate

It is never a problem to "teach" a little boy to stand to urinate. A little boy runs in while his father or a big brother is standing noisily urinating. His face lights up. "I can do that." He pulls his penis out of his pull-ups. He can spray, too! He can make a picture in the dirt. He can make a dent in the grass! He can water the back of the toilet seat. Best of all, he can watch it as he does it!

But teaching him to stand *before* he has learned to sit down to move his bowels had better be avoided. The difficulty then will be to get him to sit down at all on his potty. Once he's learned to sit, then teach him how to aim by making a noise in the toilet water or on the side of his plastic potty when he stands. He's bound to be thrilled.

I remember a little girl who watched her 4-year-old friend, a boy, stand up and pee in her backyard on a warm summer day. She wanted to try too. She took off her underpants, pulled up her dress, pulled back her shoulders, rounded her back, and stuck out her hips as far as she could. It worked! Your daughter might like to try sitting on the toilet "backward" so that she can watch her urine tinkle and splash into the toilet bowl.

Stools and Urine

Newborn babies and young infants eat and digest differently than older children. It is no wonder that their stools and urine are different too. Here are some of the differences that parents are likely to notice. They are described here in more detail than some parents might want in the hope that it will help parents feel prepared and ready for any surprise.

We of course are brought up to find body waste repelling, so many parents find themselves unexpectedly unperturbed when it comes to dealing with their own baby's urine and stools. Fathers who are hesitant to get involved with this part of their baby's care will find it far easier to overcome their discomfort if they start early.

Newborn Stool—Meconium: A newborn baby's stools are black and sticky for the first few days, and are called meconium. They are the digested contents of the uterus that the baby has swallowed over the course of pregnancy. The meconium is more or less completely discharged from the newborn baby's gut after two or three days. Any black stool after that time should be brought to your pediatrician's attention. Occasionally, a newborn may pass fresh blood in his stool that he swallowed during the delivery or later, if the mother's nipple bleeds. Even so, always report the appearance of bright red blood in your baby's bowel movements to his doctor.

After the dark, black meconium stools disappear, your baby is likely to produce greenish or yellowy curds. They are usually grainy curds containing mucus, and they are frequent. Often a newborn baby has a mucousy stool at every diaper change. Urine and stool are mixed in each diaper.

These stools are squirted with real force. A newborn baby is likely to pull up his legs, turn red, grunt, and even cry out as if in pain each time. If his anus cracks from this exertion, and you can see a bloody crack with a sliver of red blood on the diaper, wash your little finger and put petroleum jelly up into the anus ¼ of an inch to cover the crack. It should heal quickly. If not, be sure to let his doctor know.

After the first few days, stools reflect the baby's feeding. A breastfed baby is likely to have bulky, soft yellow stools many times a day. But they do not smell. I can walk into the house of a family with a newborn baby and tell by the smell of the house whether he is being breastfed or not. A breastfed baby's stools smell sweet and mild, if at all. Mustard-colored or even greenish bowel movements are common for the breastfed baby.

At around three weeks, the pattern of many breastfed newborns suddenly changes. Up until this point, they may have had as many as 8 to 10 stools a day. But at three weeks, I have seen some breastfed babies begin to produce only one stool a week. Two babies in my practice had one every ninth day, and one baby every tenth day—absolutely regularly and predictably. I gave those parents a prize for their patience.

Many parents waiting for a stool during this period wonder: "Is he OK? Should I call the doctor? He grunts and groans every day as if he wanted to go. It is all I can do not to help him with a small sliver of soap as a suppository. But if I do, he only passes gas and a tiny bit of mucus, no stool." I was able to convince many mothers in my practice that, if their babies were totally breastfed, and otherwise growing and thriving, they need not worry about infrequent stools. One mother and I weighed her baby before and after a stool we waited eight days for. He weighed four ounces (a quarter of a pound) less after his bowel movement!

The many days a breastfed baby can go without a bowel movement demonstrates to me the efficiency of breast milk. A baby can digest almost everything in it, with very little undigested residue remaining to be excreted. Babies with this pattern do extremely well. The pattern of their bowel movement timing changes again when solids are started at about 5 months.

Formula-fed babies never go for so long without a bowel movement. They should and do have regular bowel movements—often four to six a day, but at least once a day. These are often larger, bulky, pale brown, and smelly. Formula-fed babies' stools have a strong, distinctive smell. This is because babies do not fully digest the milk products in the formula. Cow's milk is made for calves, and human babies' intestines do not contain all the necessary enzymes to digest it completely.

If there is mucus or blood in your baby's stools, this may be a sign of a milk intolerance or allergy that needs to be attended to. Call your baby's doctor. If your baby starts to spit up regularly and forcefully, or if he begins to get skin rashes on his extremities or around his neck, he may need a substitute for the milk formula. It is best, though, to assess this with your pediatrician, and to make a plan together that you can carefully carry out. Too many babies are switched too soon from one formula to another, leaving everyone confused about which one caused what.

A formula-fed baby will push and squirm and turn red, just as a breastfed one will, when he has a bowel movement. If the bowel movement is at all hard, or begins to create bleeding at the anus, you will want to talk with your pediatrician about a little prune juice or a change in his formula.

Whether you give your baby breast milk or formula, you soon pay very little attention to his stools. Instead, you'll find yourself using each diaper change as an opportunity to learn about your baby. Each change gives you the chance to sing, to smile, to croon to him—and for him to learn about you. He may look at you gratefully as you change him. These opportunities become a critical part of the answer to every new parent's question: "How will I ever learn how to nurture this baby?" These many simple moments are chances for you.

Newborn Urine: Occasionally, a newborn baby's urine is reddish in color. This should disappear after the first three days, once the baby's kidneys have adjusted to the new environment outside the uterus. Wet diapers can appear as often as once an hour. If there is no urine for 4–6 hours, be sure to call your pediatrician: This is usually a sign that your baby is not drinking enough, or that he is not drinking enough to make up for fluid lost, for example, from diarrhea or vomiting (see "Diarrhea"). Sometimes, girl babies briefly pass blood from their vaginas right after birth, a sign of the influence of their mother's hormones on their tiny bodies. Don't worry.

Often mother's milk doesn't come in for four or five days. As a result, a newborn's urine will at first be sparse, and a little darker. If necessary offer extra water, and check for more frequent, lighter-colored urine once breast milk is plentiful. Urine should wet at least six diapers a day once the baby has started on breast milk or formula in earnest.

On hot days, give your baby extra water between feedings. Urine should be quite light yellow. If it turns dark, it could mean he needs more fluid. Some substances, for example, certain medications, are not digested by a small baby—and may change the urine's color. When there is any change in color in your baby's urine, be sure to call his doctor.

Training Pants
and Diaper Refusal

Wearing training pants "like a big boy" is another measure of mastery for a young child. Every toddler wants to conform in order to please others. But when conforming means being more "grown up" there is an added incentive—the toddler feels in charge of himself. Being "grown up" is a sign of this new power. No wonder he won't want to give up training pants even if there are accidents. Should you push him? I don't think so. I'd offer diapers at particularly stressful times, for trips, for night-time and naps. At the same time, you will need to respect his wish to hold on to his progress.

What can a parent do when a child refuses to go back to diapers, even at times when a diaper is likely to be needed?

1. Double the training pants;
2. Use protective coverings (for example, on his mattress, on the car seat);
3. Assure him that he can be "a big boy" in all sorts of ways, by his walk, by his clothes, by his speech;
4. Commend him for his efforts to be "grown up";
5. When he is wearing training pants, reassure him that he can pull them down himself, change them himself, even drop them in the dirty laundry hamper by himself.

He is trying so hard to be "a big boy."

Travel and Toilet Training

Whenever you travel with a child who is just beginning to understand the idea of urinating and moving his bowels in a certain place, you are likely to disrupt his learning. As he first grasps the idea of toilet training he is likely to think that only his own potty (or the toilets in his home) will do: "This is where I go poo and pee. Like mommy. Like daddy." He is proud of his successful imitation of those he looks up to most.

But when you travel with a child who has not yet been fully toilet trained, you are introducing a whole new idea. To master it, he will need to wonder, "Do mommy and daddy go to a different place to do their poo? I'm scared to try that. What if I can't do it?" The routine he has learned at home—of fitting into his parents' patterns—is likely to break down. He will be likely to fail, at first—and to be surprised and vulnerable when he loses their newfound approval for all he has learned at home.

Many children need the reassuring familiarity of a routine or ritual to go with their early efforts to use the potty. Going to the potty each time in the same place, with the same teddy bear to hold, or the same book to read, makes it easier for them to concentrate on this new task. Initially, a young child is likely to hold on to these rituals rigidly, insisting: "I need to go in the same place. In *my* potty. Like *my* daddy. At *my* house." It may have taken awhile for him to learn to give up his poops to the potty. Asking him to produce his important excretions outside of his ritual spots may be difficult at first. Don't push. Let him decide

What To Do—If You
Must Travel During Toilet Training

1. Prepare the child ahead of time, "We're going to a special new place. There will be new toilets there. But don't worry. We can bring your own potty, and some diapers too, if you need them."
2. Take along a potty he has used before.
3. Let him know that you understand that the important bathroom rituals you and he have set up will be disrupted. He is bound to feel stressed by the changes in the routine that he has tried hard to conform to.
4. "You can wear your training pants for this big trip if you want. Then you won't have to worry about whether you always make it to the toilet or not." Permission to "fail"—and recognition of the big adjustment you are asking him to make—are both important.
5. Let him know you are confident, and that there is plenty of time: "When we come back, we can start over again."
6. Be sure to respect the fact that his productions—his bowel movements and urine—need to be treated as if they were precious. Your child may not be ready for you to flush them away in a new place—like grandma's toilet or a hotel bathroom. Instead, praise him when he urinates or after a bowel movement, and ask him whether he wants to wait to flush it way. Once he's ready he can be proud that now he can flush new toilets wherever he goes.

where and when he will cooperate. It must be kept as his achievement, not yours.

Before going off to school, or on a trip, or to visit others, you may gently suggest that he try his potty first, even mentioning that you know how much he likes to use his own. You could try picking out a "travel" potty with him for him to take to school and on trips. Help him feel that it is as special as his "home" potty. Or encourage him to take his favorite potty time book with him to read, or his favorite teddy bear who can go poo too when he needs to go away from home.

Don't be surprised when a child who has already mastered toilet training has an accident on a trip. He may not be sure where the toilet is. He may not know how much time to leave himself to get there before it is too late. Or when he gets there, he may be uncomfortable about sitting on a strange new toilet, and flushing his productions to some strange new place. He's bound to hold back, and then go later, in his pants. He may also regress with an accident as a reaction to the changes—different people, place, and schedule—that come with travel.

Don't make a fuss about it. Instead, your child will need your reassurance that "accidents happen to everybody."

Urinary Infections

If a child begins to complain of burning on urination, urinates much more frequently (even waking at night to urinate), or complains of pain in the area of the bladder (below the belly button) or the genitals, look out for a urinary tract infection. A urinary tract infection occurs when bacteria enter and multiply inside the bladder or kidneys. A child with a urinary tract infection may also start wetting the bed again, or dribble urine. He may also complain of back pain.

Such an infection may be less obvious in an infant, who won't be able to tell you about the pain, and is likely to have less specific symptoms: irritability, trouble feeding, vomiting, diarrhea. Both infants and older children with urinary tract infections may have fever, a distinctive odor to the urine, and even blood in the urine.

Little girls, who are more prone to urinary tract infections (UTIs) than boys, also may develop a mild irritation of the vagina. If your female toddler complains only of discomfort around her vagina, you may first want to check for such an irritation. Gently spread her vagina apart while you sing or talk to her to distract her. If the skin looks raw and red, it may just be a vaginal irritation, which is common and usually not serious. Apply A&D ointment or petroleum jelly gently with your forefinger with each diaper change. You may, though, want to show it to your baby's doctor, because such irritations can also be caused by thrush (*Candida*) and they will need a special kind of ointment (see "Diaper Rash").

If a child complains of a burning pain while urinating, or if you notice that he is urinating more frequently than usual for more than a day, you should let your pediatrician know. He or she may ask you to wash the baby's genital area off gently so that you can then catch a "clean specimen" for your doctor. You'll need a special, sterilized container to catch the urine. You can put this little jar, with the cover off (don't touch the insides), inside a flat pan, and then set your child on the pan when he's about to urinate. Take the sample to the doctor as soon as you can, while it is fresh. If your child has a urinary infection, it should show up in the doctor's tests. Under a microscope, many white blood cells indicate an infection in the urinary tract.

Little girls who have urinary tract infections once are more likely to have them again. These infections can be treated effectively with antibiotics. Cranberry juice can help too, since the bacteria are sensitive to the acid in it. But it won't do the job by itself. If your child can't stand the taste of the antibiotics, find out from your doctor or pharmacist if there is some food or drink you can safely mix it with—but you'll have to make sure your child swallows the entire dose each time.

Always be sure your child takes the antibiotic medicine for the full length of time the doctor has prescribed. Otherwise, a few bacteria may be left in the bladder to start growing again, setting up another episode of infection. Worse still, the leftover bacteria are more likely to be resistant to the antibiotic so that the next round of infection may be more difficult to treat.

Your doctor should ask for another urine specimen after your child has taken all the medicine in order to be sure that the infection has been completely wiped out. A long-lasting infection can damage a child's kidneys, but with good treatment this can usually be avoided.

Urinary tract infections themselves can often be prevented in girls by being sure that they learn to wipe themselves from front to back, *never* back to front, so that bacteria from the anus are not spread to the urinary tract. Bacteria that normally live in human stool do not disturb the digestive tract and anus, but they can cause infection if they are introduced into the urinary tract (at the opening just above a little girl's vagina, or at the tip of a little boy's penis).

Urinary infections are far less common in males. They also need to be treated and followed for any evidence of lingering infection. A burning sensation while urinating and increased frequency of urination call for a urinalysis.

Your child's doctor may decide to look for reasons why a urinary tract infection has occurred in a young boy. Frequent urination (more than eight to ten times a day) can be a sign of diabetes: A urinalysis can also detect the excess sugar in the urine caused by diabetes. Any child, boy or girl, who has recurrent urinary tract infections will need a careful assessment by a pediatrician to look for the underlying reason. Since these infections are so rare in males, many pediatricians will want to do more tests (for example, X-rays or ultrasounds) to be sure there isn't an abnormality of the urinary system that needs treatment. Certainly by the second infection, a boy should receive such additional attention.

Appendix

Books for Children

Capucilli, Alyssa Satin. *The Potty Book for Boys*. New York: Barron's Publishers, 2000.

Capucilli, Alyssa Satin. *The Potty Book for Girls*. New York: Barron's Publishers, 2000.

Cho, Shinta (Amanda Mayer Stinchecum, translator). *The Gas We Pass: The Story of Farts*. La Jolla, Calif.: Kane/Miller Publishers, 1994.

Frankel, Alona. *Once Upon a Potty*. New York: Harper Collins, 1988.

Gomi, Taro (Amanda Mayer Stinchecum, translator). *Everyone Poops*. La Jolla, Calif: Kane/Miller Publishers, 1993.

Sanschagrin, Joceline. *Caillou Potty Time*. Montreal: Chouette, 2000.

Books for Parents

Brazelton, T. B. *Touchpoints: Your Child's Emotional and Behavioral Development*. Cambridge, Mass.: Addison–Wesley, 1992.

Brazelton, T. B., and Sparrow, J. D. *Discipline: The Brazelton Way.* Cambridge, Mass.: Perseus Books, 2003.

Brazelton, T. B., and Sparrow, J. D. *Feeding Your Child: The Brazelton Way.* Cambridge, Mass.: Da Capo Press, 2004.

Brazelton, T. B., and Sparrow, J. D. *Sleep: The Brazelton Way.* Cambridge, Mass.: Perseus Books, 2003.

Brazelton, T. B., and Sparrow, J. D. *Touchpoints Three to Six: Your Child's Emotional and Behavioral Development.* Cambridge, Mass.: Perseus Books, 2001.

Children's Hospital Boston, Woolf, Alan, Kenna, Margaret, and Shane, Howard, Eds. *Children's Hospital Guide to Your Child's Health and Development.* Cambridge, Mass.: Perseus Books, 2001.

Dixon, Suzanne, and Stein, Martin, Eds. *Encounters with Children.* Chicago/London: Year Book Medical Publishers, 1987.

Eisenburg, A., Markoff, H., and Hathaway, S. E., Eds. *What to Expect in the Toddler Years.* New York: Workman Publishing Company, 1994.

Leach, Penelope. *Your Baby and Child: From Birth to Age Five.* New York: Knopf, 1997.

Wolraich, Mark L., Ed. *American Academy of Pediatrics Guide to Toilet Training.* New York: Bantam Books, 2003.

References for Professionals (including "classic" papers)

Bell, A. I., and Levine, M. L. "The Psychologic Aspects of Pediatric Practice: I. Causes and Treatment of Chronic Constipation," in *Pediatrics* 14(259) (1954).

Blum, N. J., Taubman, B., and Nemeth, N. "Relationship Between Age at Initiation of Toilet Training and Duration of Training: A Prospective Study," in *Pediatrics* 111(4), 810–814, 2003.

Brazelton, T. B. "A Child Oriented Approach to Toilet Training," in *Pediatrics* 29, 121–128 (1962).

Bromfeld, J. M., and Douglas, J. W. "Bedwetting Prevalence Among Children Aged 4–7 years," in *Lancet* 270, 850 (1956).

Byrd, R. S., Weitzman, M., Lamphear, N. E., and Auinger, P. "Bedwetting in US Children: Epidemiology and Related Behavior Problems," in *Pediatrics* 98(3), 414–419 (1996).

Davidson, M. "Constipation and Fecal Incontinence," in *Pediatric Clinics of North America* 5, 749 (1958).

Fishman, L., Rappaport, L., Couisneau, D., and Nurko, S. "Early Constipation and Toilet Training in Children with Encopresis," in *Journal of Pediatric Gastroenterology and Nutrition* 34(4), 385–388 (2002).

Hoeckelman, R. A., Adam, H. M., Nelson, N. M., Weitzman, M. L., and Wilson, M. H. *Primary Pediatric Care.* St. Louis: Mosby, 2001.

Huschka, M. "Child's Response to Coercive Bowel Training," in *Psychosomatic Medicine* 4, 301 (1942).

Kawaguchi, A., Tanaka, Y., Yamao, Y., et al. "Follow-up Study of Bedwetting from Three–Five Years," in *Urology* 58(5), 772–776 (2001).

Neveus, T., Hetta, S. Cnattingius, S., et al. "Depth of Sleep and Sleep Habits Among Enuretic and Incontinent Children," in *Acta Paediatrica* 88(7), 748–752 (1991).

Prugh, D. "Childhood Experience and Colonic Disorders," in *Annals of New York Academy of Science* 58, 355 (1954).

Resources for Parents

American Academy of Pediatrics
P.O. Box 927
Elk Grove Village, Ill. 60009
(847) 434-4000
www.aap.org

American Pseudo-Obstruction and Hirschsprung's Disease Society
158 Pleasant St.
North Andover, Mass. 01845–2797
(978) 685–4477
Fax: (978) 685–4488
www.tiac.net/users.aphs

National Digestive Disease Information Clearinghouse
National Institute of Diabetes and Digestive and Kidney Diseases
2 Information Way
Bethesda, Md. 20892–3570
(301) 654–3810
Fax: (301) 907–8906
www.niddk.nih.gov

Zero to Three
2000 M St., NW, Suite 200
Washington, D.C. 20036
www.zerotothree.org

Toilet School
Brazelton Touchpoint Center
Children's Hospital Boston
1295 Boylston St., Suite 320
Boston, Mass. 02115

Videotapes

Brazelton, T. B. *Toilet Training Your Child.* Boston: Brazelton Foundation.
Frankel, Alona. *Once Upon a Potty for Her.* Boston Educational, 1990.
Frankel, Alona. *Once Upon a Potty for Him.* Boston Educational, 1990.

Acknowledgments

We would like to thank parents across the country for having first urged us to write these concise, accessible books on topics of the utmost importance to them, for without their vision they might never have been written. Thanks too go to Geoffrey Canada, Marilyn Joseph, and the Baby College staff, and to Bart and Karen Lawson, David Saltzman, and Caressa Singleton for their unwavering support for our work, and from whom we have learned so much. We thank Ann Stadtler for sharing her wisdom and insights from "Toilet School" at Children's Hospital Boston and for her thoughtful review of this manuscript. As always we would again like to thank our editor, Merloyd Lawrence, for her wisdom and guidance. Finally, we wish to express our gratitude to our families, not only for their encouragement and patience, but for the lessons they have taught us that we have sought to impart in this book.

Index

About the Authors

T. Berry Brazelton, M.D., founder of the Child Development Unit at Children's Hospital Boston, is Clinical Professor of Pediatrics Emeritus at Harvard Medical School. His many important and popular books include the internationally best-selling *Touchpoints* and *Infants and Mothers.* A practicing pediatrician for over forty-five years, Dr. Brazelton has also created the Brazelton Foundation (www.brazeltonfoundation.org) to support child development training for healthcare and educational professionals around the world.

Joshua D. Sparrow, M.D., is Assistant Professor of Psychiatry at Harvard Medical School and Special Initiatives Director at the Brazelton Touchpoints Center. He is the co-author, with Dr. Brazelton, of *Touchpoints Three to Six, Calming Your Fussy Baby: The Brazelton Way, Discipline: The Brazelton Way, Feeding Your Child: The Brazelton Way,* and *Sleep: The Brazelton Way.*